Kono Ikehara

The Japanese Secret to Happiness and Success

IKIGAI

"Rediscover your purpose, live with intention,
and turn your passions into opportunities for a life full
of meaning and harmony."

Copyright © 2025 Kono Ikehara.
All rights reserved.

This book, or any part of it, may not be reproduced, distributed, or transmitted in any form or by any means, including photocopying, recording, or other electronic or mechanical methods, without the explicit written permission of the author, except as permitted by copyright law.

Short quotations or references to the text may be used for academic, journalistic, or review purposes, provided proper attribution is given to the author and the original work.

This book is a work protected by copyright law. Any similarities to actual persons, living or deceased, places, events, or locations are purely coincidental and not intended to represent reality.

Introduction

Why write a book about Ikigai?

In today's fast-paced world, filled with constant pressures, more and more people find themselves asking: "What is the true purpose of my life?" This universal question—so simple yet deeply complex—is at the heart of the Japanese philosophy of Ikigai. And it is precisely why I decided to write this book.

Ikigai is not a passing trend nor a shallow solution for those seeking easy answers. It is an ancient philosophy deeply rooted in Japanese culture, capable of uniting mind, body, heart, and soul in profound balance. Ikigai doesn't merely promise happiness; instead, it offers a path to discovering who we truly are, living with intention, and finding joy in the small moments of everyday life. This book was born out of a desire to share this timeless wisdom with you, adapting it to today's realities without compromising its essence. Through theoretical reflections, practical exercises, and inspiring stories, I aim to guide you on your journey toward discovering your Ikigai.

The universal need to find purpose in life

Every human being longs to feel part of something greater, to contribute to the world in a meaningful way, and, above all, to live a life that feels purposeful. Yet, in modern society, it's easy to lose our way. Work, social expectations, family responsibilities, and the daily rush often pull us away from what truly matters.

Many people find themselves suspended between the frustration of not knowing where they're headed and the deep desire to change course. Perhaps, as you read these lines, you too feel a need for clarity, harmony, and a direction that reflects who you truly are.

Ikigai is the answer to this search. It's not about chasing unattainable ideals but about uncovering the hidden beauty in your daily life, living authentically, and embracing a life full of meaning. How to use this book: theory and practice to transform your life. This book is designed to be much more than a theoretical read. It's a practical guide, meant to inspire you and help you turn ideas into concrete actions.

Each chapter will bring you closer to discovering your Ikigai, offering:

- **Theoretical knowledge**: to understand the origins, pillars, and benefits of Ikigai.
- **Practical exercises**: to explore yourself, identify your most authentic desires, and integrate Ikigai into your daily life.
- **Real and inspiring stories**: to provide concrete examples of people living according to their Ikigai.

There is no single path to Ikigai, as each individual is unique. My goal is to provide you with the tools you need to build your own path, step by step.

I conclude this introduction with an invitation: approach this book with an open mind and a heart ready to embrace new possibilities. Ikigai is not a destination to reach, but a journey to undertake with curiosity and dedication.

Are you ready to discover who you truly are?

Theoretical Part

The Theory of Ikigai

Chapter 1

What is Ikigai

"Happiness is nothing more than the scent of our purpose."

—Antoine de Saint-Exupéry —

The Origin and Meaning of the Word Ikigai

The word Ikigai is a Japanese term composed of two fundamental elements:

iki (口き), meaning "to live" or "life," and gai (甲斐), which can be translated as "value," "worth," or "reason." Together, the expression suggests "a reason to live" or "what makes life worth living." However, as often happens with words rooted in deep cultural significance, the meaning of Ikigai goes far beyond a simple literal translation. In Japan, the idea of Ikigai represents something deeply personal and intimate. It is not a fixed or singular concept; rather, it manifests as a subjective experience, unique to each individual. For some, Ikigai might be found in their work or a passion turned into a vocation; for others, it resides in personal relationships, acts of kindness, or simply enjoying the small pleasures of daily life, such as a cup of tea in the morning or watching a sunset through the window.

The Cultural Roots of Ikigai

To fully understand Ikigai, it is necessary to immerse oneself in Japanese culture—a culture that has always valued a sense of purpose and the deep connection between the individual and the community. The philosophy of Ikigai has its origins in ancient Japanese traditions that promote harmony and respect for the cycle of life.

A concept closely related to Ikigai is wa (和), which means "harmony." In the Japanese context, harmony is not simply the absence of conflict but a subtle balance between different aspects of life: work, relationships, personal well-being, and contributing to collective welfare. Ikigai lies precisely within this balance, acting as a driving force that encourages individuals to live with intention and fullness.

Moreover, Ikigai is intrinsically tied to community and a sense of belonging. In the small villages of Okinawa—a region renowned for the exceptional longevity of its inhabitants—Ikigai is often attributed to the concept of moai, or social connections that provide mutual support and a sense of purpose in daily life. For these communities, having a purpose is not just an individual matter but a shared responsibility that contributes to collective well-being.

A Timeless Concept

Although Ikigai is deeply rooted in Japanese culture, its relevance extends far beyond the borders of this nation. In an era marked by frenetic and often alienating lifestyles, the idea of finding a reason to live has gained new universality. However, it is important to emphasize that Ikigai is not a modern concept nor a passing trend. Its roots stretch back centuries, to a time when the Japanese began developing a worldview that emphasized the connection between individual purpose and the meaning of life.

A fascinating historical reference can be found in the Heian period (794–1185), an era of extraordinary cultural development in Japan. During this time, the term gai was already used to describe something that brought value or satisfaction to life. Over time, the meaning of gai evolved, merging with iki to create a broader and more universal concept.

Another element that has shaped the idea of Ikigai is Buddhism, particularly Zen Buddhism. Zen philosophy highlights the importance of the present moment, living with mindfulness, and seeking inner balance—all elements reflected in the essence of Ikigai. The ability to find joy in small things, such as the simple act of tending to a garden or preparing a meal, is a key principle shared by both Zen and Ikigai.

Ikigai and Happiness: A Different Approach

In Western culture, the concept of happiness is often tied to material success or the achievement of long-term goals. Ikigai, however, offers a different perspective: it's not about chasing grand milestones but about appreciating what you already have and living each day with gratitude and intention. It's a form of happiness rooted in being rather than having.

For example, an elderly fisherman in Okinawa might find his Ikigai in the daily routine of heading out to sea at sunrise, feeling the wind on his face and the waves beneath his feet. It's not about accumulating wealth or recognition but about living in harmony with oneself and the surrounding environment.

Ikigai: A Compass for Modern Life.

In today's modern society, marked by multitasking, stress, and a constant sense of dissatisfaction, the concept of Ikigai can serve as a compass to help rediscover one's direction. It's not about abandoning work or responsibilities but about reconnecting with what truly motivates and energizes us. For some, Ikigai might be a job they love; for others, it could be a hobby, a creative activity, or simply the act of caring for others. What makes Ikigai so powerful is its flexibility: there is no single, universal formula. Your Ikigai is deeply personal, evolving over time and shifting through the different stages of your life. It's a continuous journey rather than a final destination.

Ikigai as a Japanese Philosophy of Life

More than just an abstract idea, Ikigai represents a true philosophy of life for many Japanese people. It is a concept that extends beyond theory, permeating daily life, guiding choices, behaviors, and the way one approaches life. In Japan, Ikigai is not seen as a goal to be achieved but as a continuous process—a practice that unfolds in every moment. It is the invisible thread that connects individual meaning to the collective, creating a full and harmonious existence.

Ikigai and Intentional Living

At the heart of the Ikigai philosophy lies the concept of intentional living. This means being fully present in the moment while also making decisions that reflect your values and purpose. It's not about acting out of habit or automation but about consciously choosing how to invest your time and energy.

In a modern world that constantly pushes us toward material goals and external standards of success, Ikigai invites us to pause and reflect on what truly matters to us.For example, many Japanese people find their Ikigai in seemingly simple activities, such as tending to a garden, caring for their family, or pursuing a hobby they are passionate about. These activities, while they may appear small or insignificant to those chasing grand achievements, are viewed as fundamental to building a fulfilling life. It is precisely in these small, everyday actions that Ikigai comes to life.

Ikigai and the Importance of Community

A key aspect of the Ikigai philosophy is the sense of belonging to a community. In Japanese culture, the individual is never completely separate from the group; on the contrary, there is a strong connection between personal well-being and collective well-being. This is reflected in the concept of moai, which is particularly prevalent among the residents of Okinawa, one of the regions where Ikigai is most deeply rooted. A moai is a social support group, often made up of friends or neighbors, who gather regularly to share moments, support one another, and celebrate life. In these communities, Ikigai is not merely an individual matter; it is deeply intertwined with human relationships and the contributions each person can make to others. Living with Ikigai means recognizing that personal happiness and purpose are inextricably linked to the well-being of the community. This connection between Ikigai and community is particularly significant in an era when many people, especially in the West, suffer from social isolation. The Japanese philosophy reminds us that our purpose is not found solely within ourselves but also in the relationships we nurture and the ways we contribute to the world around us.

Ikigai and Simplicity

Another pillar of Ikigai as a philosophy of life is simplicity. The Japanese have a profound respect for the beauty of simple and natural things—a sensitivity that is also reflected in other Japanese philosophies, such as Wabi-Sabi (the art of finding beauty in imperfection) and Zen. Living according to Ikigai means learning to see the value and beauty in the ordinary moments of life rather than constantly chasing grand achievements or extraordinary successes.

This simplicity is not synonymous with deprivation but with mindfulness. It is about letting go of the unnecessary to focus on what truly matters. It is an approach that fosters gratitude, respect for the present, and a deep connection with nature. In this sense, Ikigai is not only a guide to finding purpose but also an invitation to live with greater lightness and authenticity.

Ikigai and Resilience

Resilience is another fundamental aspect of Ikigai. In Japanese culture, life is seen as a journey of highs and lows, and Ikigai helps individuals find their center even during difficult times. No matter how unfavorable circumstances may seem, those who live with Ikigai understand that their purpose can serve as a source of inner strength. For instance, many stories of longevity from Okinawa reveal how Ikigai helped individuals overcome wars, poverty, and other hardships. In these narratives, their personal purpose—whether it was caring for loved ones, working the land, or passing down cultural traditions—provided them with a reason to persevere even in the darkest moments. This philosophy encourages viewing challenges not as insurmountable obstacles but as opportunities to grow and strengthen one's connection to what truly matters.

Ikigai and the Balance of Mind, Body, and Spirit

An essential element of Ikigai is its holistic approach. Living with Ikigai means achieving a harmonious balance between mind, body, and spirit. This balance is cultivated by leading a life that reflects one's values and passions, while also caring for one's physical and emotional well-being.

The Japanese place great importance on health and longevity, and this is evident in their lifestyles. Activities such as meditation, practicing martial arts, or even simply taking a walk in nature are considered tools to nurture one's Ikigai. Similarly, following a balanced diet and sharing meals with loved ones are integral parts of a purposeful life.

Conclusion

Ikigai as a Japanese philosophy of life is far more than a theoretical concept. It is a daily practice that invites us to live with intention, cultivate meaningful relationships, and find beauty in simplicity. It serves as a guide for facing life with resilience and gratitude, reminding us that our purpose is not found in a distant destination but in the small actions and choices we make every day.

Why Ikigai is Important in Modern Society

We live in an era of profound complexity, marked by a fast pace and ever-growing expectations. Modern society, with its endless possibilities and pressures, provides many opportunities but also fosters a pervasive sense of dissatisfaction, anxiety, and disorientation. In this context, the concept of Ikigai emerges as a powerful and necessary response. This Japanese philosophy, which invites us to find our purpose in life and embrace a meaningful and fulfilling existence, is more relevant than ever.

The Absence of Purpose: A Problem of Our Time

One of the primary issues afflicting contemporary society is the lack of purpose. Despite technological advancements, material comforts, and unprecedented access to information, many people feel lost. The phenomenon of burnout, workplace alienation, and the rise in stress-related disorders are just a few symptoms of this widespread malaise.Professionally, work is often perceived as a source of frustration rather than a means of self-expression. On a personal level, many struggle to form meaningful connections, trapped in superficial relationships or lifestyles that prioritize competition over cooperation. In this landscape, Ikigai offers an alternative: a tool to rediscover a sense of purpose, connection, and harmony

Ikigai and Work: A New Perspective

Modern society often defines a person's worth by their professional success. However, this approach frequently overlooks inner well-being and an individual's true desires. Ikigai offers a different paradigm: work is not merely a means to earn a living but can become an integral part of a meaningful life.

Ikigai is based on a balance between four elements: what you love, what you are good at, what the world needs, and what you can be paid for. This balance is particularly relevant in modern society, where many people find themselves in jobs they do not enjoy or that they perceive as meaningless. Through Ikigai, individuals can reflect on how to integrate passion, vocation, and profession, making work a source of fulfillment rather than just stress.

For instance, someone working in a creative field but feeling financial pressure could use Ikigai to find a balance between artistic expression and financial sustainability. Similarly, a professional dissatisfied with their current role might discover that their true Ikigai lies in an entirely different activity, such as teaching, traveling, or starting a personal project.

The Need for Connection and Belonging

In an increasingly interconnected world, the paradox of isolation is striking. Despite the ability to communicate with anyone at any time, many people suffer from loneliness and a lack of authentic relationships. Ikigai emphasizes the importance of belonging and community as fundamental pillars of a meaningful life.

This connection doesn't necessarily need to involve large groups of people. For many, Ikigai is found in caring for family, building lasting friendships, or participating in small local communities. The simple act of sharing time and energy with others can create a sense of purpose that goes far beyond the pursuit of individual goals.Modern society, with its focus on individualism and competition, often undervalues the power of relationships. Ikigai reminds us that we are not isolated islands but part of a larger social fabric, and finding meaning in life also involves contributing to the well-being of others.

Ikigai and Mental Well-Being: An Antidote to Stress

Modern life is often accompanied by high levels of stress and anxiety. Economic uncertainty, work pressures, and constant exposure to social media can create feelings of inadequacy and insecurity. Ikigai offers an approach to counter these feelings, promoting inner calm and resilience.

One of the fundamental principles of Ikigai is awareness of the present moment. This practice, akin to mindfulness, helps people focus on what truly matters, reducing the burden of unnecessary worries. Additionally, Ikigai encourages viewing each day as an opportunity to grow and contribute, turning even the most difficult challenges into chances for learning. For instance, someone experiencing work-related anxiety might find that dedicating time to a beloved hobby or a social cause helps reduce stress and restore balance. Ikigai doesn't eliminate problems but helps change perspective, making them easier to face.

Ikigai and Sustainability: A Model for the Future

Another significant aspect of Ikigai in modern society relates to sustainability. In a world increasingly aware of environmental and social crises, Ikigai can provide a guide for living more intentionally and responsibly. The philosophy of Ikigai encourages reflection on how personal purpose can contribute to the collective good, promoting a lifestyle that respects the planet and future generations.

For example, someone might discover their Ikigai in teaching environmental education, supporting disadvantaged communities, or creating innovative projects that blend ethics with entrepreneurship. This approach not only enriches the individual's life but also helps to build a more balanced and harmonious world.

Conclusion

Ikigai is important in modern society because it addresses many of the challenges we face today: the lack of purpose, social isolation, stress, and the need for sustainability. It is not a universal or immediate solution but a philosophy that invites us to explore our personal meaning, build authentic connections, and live with awareness. This Japanese philosophy, rooted in centuries of wisdom, offers a powerful message: each of us can find our purpose and live a life that not only holds value but also contributes to the world's well-being. In Ikigai, there is no perfection, but there is the key to navigating the complexities of our time.

What You Love to Do (Passion)

The first pillar of Ikigai, what you love to do, represents the core of a life lived with purpose and meaning. This element refers to the activities that ignite you, that fill you with enthusiasm, and allow you to connect with the most authentic part of yourself. When you truly do something you love, time seems to pass effortlessly, and your effort becomes natural, even joyful.

Discovering what you love to do requires introspection and awareness, as the answer is not always immediate or obvious. Passions are not merely occasional interests or hobbies; they are an essential part of your identity. They are the activities that make you feel alive, spark your creativity, and give meaning to your days.

In a fast-paced society like ours, we often neglect what we love to do, consumed by daily responsibilities, work, or social expectations. However, nurturing your passion is the first step toward building an authentic and meaningful life.

Passion as Vital Energy

Passion is a powerful force that goes beyond mere enjoyment. It is an energy that drives you to improve, overcome difficulties, and dedicate yourself fully to what you care about. For instance, a musician might spend hours playing their instrument—not because they have to, but because they find deep satisfaction in the act of playing. Similarly, a gardener might spend entire days tending to plants, feeling connected to nature and the cycle of life.

This deep connection to what you do is one of the main indicators that you are following your passion. When you engage in an activity you love, you experience the so-called flow state: a condition of total immersion where time seems to stop and every action flows naturally. This state is not only rewarding but also beneficial for your mental and emotional well-being.

Discovering What You Love to Do

Many people struggle to identify what they truly love to do because the fast pace of modern life often leaves little room for reflection. However, finding your passion is a crucial step toward uncovering your Ikigai. The process of discovery takes time and introspection, but it can be guided by asking yourself a few key questions:

- What excites you? Which activities make you feel energized and full of vitality?
- What would you do even if you weren't being paid for it? Passions aren't born from seeking material rewards but from the intrinsic joy of the activity itself.
- What did you enjoy doing as a child? Often, our most authentic interests emerge during childhood, before external pressures influence our choices.
- What do you do purely for the sake of doing it? Reflect on activities you engage in with no practical purpose, simply because they bring you pleasure.
- What topics excite you in conversations? The things you discuss enthusiastically are often clues to your deepest passions.

Answering these questions doesn't always lead to an immediate revelation, but it can give you a starting point for exploring what truly inspires you.

The Challenges of Cultivating Passion

Even when you discover what you love to do, finding the time or space to nurture it can be difficult. Work, family, or financial responsibilities often pull us away from what brings us joy. However, Ikigai teaches us that dedicating time to your passions is not a luxury but a necessity for your well-being.

For example, a young professional with a passion for writing may find it hard to devote time to creativity after long workdays. Yet, even dedicating just 30 minutes a day to writing can make a significant difference—not only by improving skills but also by bringing a sense of fulfillment to daily life. Passions don't need to become a job or career to hold value. You can cultivate them in small steps, integrating them into your routine without upending your lifestyle. Even a brief moment spent doing what you love can positively impact your mood and energy.

Passion and Meaning

Passion isn't just a source of pleasure; it's a path to giving meaning to your life. When we engage in what we love, we don't just experience temporary happiness—we feel deeply connected to who we are and to the world around us. Passion allows us to express our true selves, recognize our place in the world, and contribute to the well-being of others. Through passion, we find a purpose that extends beyond ourselves, becoming part of something greater.

Passion as Self-Expression

Doing what you love is one of the most authentic ways to express who you truly are. When you follow a passion, you're not merely engaging in an activity; you're manifesting your values, interests, and unique character. For example, someone who loves painting isn't just creating artwork—they are transforming thoughts, emotions, and perceptions into art, making their inner world visible.

This process not only enriches your life but also allows you to communicate with others in a genuine and meaningful way. Passion becomes a means of exploring and defining your identity. The more you nurture what you love, the more you learn about yourself—what excites you, what motivates you, and what makes you unique. This process of self-discovery is fundamental to building a life filled with meaning.

Contribution to the Well-Being of Others

Passion isn't just a personal experience; it also has the potential to enrich the lives of those around us. When you dedicate yourself to something you love, your enthusiasm becomes contagious, inspiring others.

Moreover, many passions have a direct impact on the community or the world at large. For example, a teacher who loves their work isn't just imparting knowledge—they're transmitting energy, curiosity, and motivation to their students. This not only enhances the educational experience but can also positively influence the students' futures, helping them discover their own passions and believe in their abilities.

Similarly, a volunteer who dedicates their time to a social cause finds meaning not only in the act of volunteering itself but also in the tangible outcomes of their efforts. Whether it's helping those in need, supporting environmental protection, or contributing to a community project, the volunteer feels that their actions make a real impact. This sense of purpose strengthens the connection between passion and meaning, showing how what you love can become a service to others.

The Multiplier Effect of Passion

An often-overlooked aspect of passion is its multiplier effect. When you do what you love, your energy and enthusiasm inspire others to do the same. For instance, an entrepreneur passionate about their idea can motivate employees to believe in the project, creating a positive and productive work environment. Similarly, a musician performing with passion can move the audience, encouraging listeners to reflect, dream, or embark on new paths in their own lives. This multiplier effect demonstrates that passion is never confined to a purely personal dimension. It has the potential to create change not only in your life but also in the lives of others. This makes passion one of the most powerful forces for bringing meaning to existence.

Overcoming Difficulties Through Passion

Another crucial connection between passion and meaning is found in the ability to face life's challenges and difficulties. When you dedicate yourself to something you love, you find a deep motivation to overcome obstacles. Passion provides energy even during tough times, helping you maintain resilience and determination.

For instance, an athlete who loves their sport endures hard training sessions, injuries, and competitions with a positive spirit because they are driven by their passion for what they do. Even when results aren't immediate or sacrifices feel burdensome, the sense of meaning derived from passion serves as a guiding light, illuminating the path forward.

Integrating Passion Into Daily Life

Cultivating passion doesn't necessarily mean overhauling your life or turning it into a career. Often, the most profound moments of meaning arise from the ability to integrate what you love into your daily routine. Even small actions, like spending 30 minutes a day reading a book you enjoy, practicing a musical instrument, or spending time in nature, can greatly enrich your life. The key is to treat your passions as a priority rather than relegating them to a marginal activity. When you make space for what you love, your sense of meaning grows, positively influencing other aspects of your life, such as work, relationships, and personal well-being.

Conclusion

Passion is one of the keys to finding meaning in life. It not only allows you to connect with yourself and express your true self but also has the potential to inspire and enrich the lives of others. Whether you are a teacher, an artist, a volunteer, or simply someone who quietly nurtures their passions, what you love to do can become a transformative force. Integrating passion into your daily life is an essential step toward your Ikigai. No matter how big or small your passion may be, cultivating it with dedication and intentionality will help you live a more authentic, happy, and meaningful life.

What You're Good At (Vocation)

The second pillar of Ikigai, what you're good at, refers to your skills, talents, and abilities that you have developed throughout your life. This aspect, also known as vocation, is what enables you to excel in certain activities and contribute uniquely to the world around you. While passion focuses on what you love to do, vocation adds another essential element: the recognition and development of your innate and acquired abilities. Finding what you're good at means discovering and honing your strengths, identifying areas for improvement, and leveraging your skills to create value. It's not just about what you can do well, but about what you can do with intention and dedication to achieve meaningful results. This pillar not only enriches your personal life but can also open new professional and social opportunities.

The Connection Between Talent and Vocation

Each of us possesses innate talents, but we often fail to recognize or fully develop them. Vocation is what emerges when these abilities are nurtured and transformed into something tangible. For example, someone with a natural inclination for empathy might excel in professions that require relational skills, such as teaching, counseling, or social support. Similarly, someone with strong creativity might find their vocation in design, art, or technological innovation.

It's important to note that what you're good at isn't always something you discover right away. Many skills emerge through experience, practice, and continuous learning. For instance, someone might discover their talent for writing only after starting to keep a journal or occasionally contributing articles. This demonstrates that vocation isn't a starting point but a process of discovery and development.

Discovering What You're Good At

Identifying your skills and talents requires honest reflection and a bit of exploration. Here are some helpful questions to better understand what you're good at:

- **What activities come naturally to you?**

- Are there things you do easily and effortlessly compared to others? These might be clues to your innate abilities.

- **What do others ask you for help with?**

Often, people around us recognize our talents before we do. If friends, colleagues, or family turn to you for specific tasks or advice, it's likely you have skills in that area.

- **What have you learned to do over time?**

Not all talents are innate; many are developed through study, practice, and experience. Reflect on what you've gained along your personal and professional journey.

- **What results have you achieved?**

Looking at your past successes can provide insights into what you excel at. Whether it's a well-executed work project, a hobby taken to an advanced level, or a personal goal achieved, each accomplishment reveals something about your abilities.

- What challenges you but motivates you to improve?

Sometimes, what you're good at isn't fully developed yet but lies in activities that require effort and continuous growth.

Developing Your Skills

Recognizing what you're good at is only the beginning of your journey toward Ikigai. For vocation to reach its full potential, you need to invest time, dedication, and effort into cultivating and refining your skills. This process doesn't happen automatically; it requires a focused plan, the courage to face new challenges, and often, the willingness to step outside your comfort zone.

The Importance of Training and Practice

The growth of your abilities inevitably requires continuous learning and practical experience. For example, an aspiring chef with a natural inclination for cooking might choose to enroll in advanced culinary courses, work under renowned chefs in high-end restaurants, or engage in personal experimentation to develop innovative recipes. Talent alone is not enough: to excel, you must refine your skills through education and consistent practice. Similarly, a professional with strong communication skills could enhance these abilities by attending public speaking workshops, learning storytelling techniques, or deepening expertise in areas such as persuasive writing or digital marketing. By exposing yourself to new contexts and seeking feedback, these skills can be transformed into highly effective tools for both personal and professional growth.

Stepping Outside Your Comfort Zone

A crucial aspect of developing your skills is the ability to embrace situations that push you beyond your usual limits. This might mean taking on a more challenging role, facing the fear of failure, or learning something entirely new.

For instance, a musician seeking to improve might decide to perform in front of a larger audience, confronting performance anxiety to build confidence and strengthen their abilities. These moments of challenge, when approached with dedication, lead not only to technical improvement but also to greater self-esteem.

Every step forward, no matter how small, helps reinforce your sense of self-worth and brings you closer to your Ikigai, allowing you to live a life where your skills align with your deepest desires and purposes.

Conclusion

Developing what you're good at is not just an investment in yourself—it's a way to build a more complete and authentic version of who you are. Every skill you refine and every step forward you take brings you closer to a meaningful and fulfilling life, where your vocation not only benefits you but also contributes to the world around you.

Putting Vocation at the Service of Others

One of the most rewarding aspects of vocation is the ability to use it to help others. Your skills are not merely tools for personal success but can become a valuable resource for your community, workplace, or the world at large. Using your abilities to serve others creates a sense of connection and belonging that enriches your life.

For example, an engineer with exceptional problem-solving skills might use their expertise to develop technological solutions that improve people's quality of life. Similarly, a therapist with excellent listening abilities can make a profound difference in the lives of those seeking help. This link between talent and social contribution is one of the most meaningful aspects of vocation.

Vocation and Personal Fulfillment

When we dedicate ourselves to what we're good at, the result is not only an improvement in the quality of what we do but also a deep sense of personal fulfillment. Vocation is more than a recognition of our skills; it represents an opportunity to put our talents to use and turn every activity into a meaningful experience.

When we invest time and energy into what we do best, we feel we are utilizing our resources to the fullest, giving deeper meaning to our daily efforts. The connection between vocation and personal fulfillment is evident in our ability to face challenges with confidence and resilience.

When we're aware of our abilities, we feel stronger when confronting obstacles because we know we have the tools to overcome them. This confidence doesn't stem from arrogance but from an understanding of our worth. For example, a doctor who knows they have excellent diagnostic skills will approach a complex case with greater determination, aware that their contribution can make a difference.

Vocation as an Expression of Potential

Vocation isn't just about doing something well—it's about how you choose to do it. It's the combination of skills, dedication, and passion that transforms ordinary work or tasks into something extraordinary. Putting your heart into what you do means infusing authenticity and meaning into your actions, elevating the value of your efforts. This approach allows you to see work not as an obligation but as an opportunity to express your potential. For example, a teacher isn't just someone who delivers knowledge; a truly dedicated teacher becomes a guide, a motivator, and an inspiration to their students. This level of commitment stems not only from technical skills but from the ability to use those skills to create a positive impact. Vocation, therefore, is not just about what you know how to do—it's about the unique way you choose to do it.

The Role of Vocation in Overcoming Challenges

When we are aligned with our vocation, the way we approach difficulties changes radically. Challenges are no longer seen as insurmountable obstacles but as opportunities to grow and further develop our abilities. Vocation provides us with an inner strength that allows us to stay focused even during the most complex times.

A concrete example might be an entrepreneur facing a period of economic crisis. If this entrepreneur is aware of their skills, such as financial management or leadership, they can use these abilities to find innovative solutions and adapt to new circumstances. Vocation not only helps to overcome challenges but also transforms difficulties into opportunities for learning and growth.

Vocation and Sense of Belonging

Another fundamental aspect of vocation is the sense of belonging it can generate. When we dedicate ourselves to what we're good at, we not only enhance our lives but also contribute to the well-being of those around us. This sense of contribution fosters a deeper connection with the community and the world at large.

For example, an engineer designing sustainable infrastructure isn't just exercising their technical skills—they're also contributing to creating a better future for society. This kind of personal fulfillment goes beyond individual satisfaction; it becomes a bridge that links our work to the collective good. Knowing that what we do has a positive impact on others further strengthens the sense of meaning in our lives.

Vocation and Long-Term Fulfillment

Vocation also plays a fundamental role in building a long-term vision for our lives. By focusing on what we're good at, we can achieve not only immediate goals but also craft a career or personal path that aligns with our values and aspirations. This process requires dedication and persistence, but the results are enduring.

For instance, a musician might start by developing their technical skills through years of practice, but true fulfillment comes when those abilities are used to create something unique, such as a musical piece that moves an audience or inspires other artists. This journey, though long and challenging, leads to satisfaction that far surpasses mere external recognition.

Conclusion

Vocation is much more than just what we're good at—it's a way to build an authentic and meaningful life. When we pour our hearts and skills into what we do, work becomes an expression of our potential and a means to leave a mark on the world. Through vocation, we not only find personal fulfillment but also create value for others, generating a positive impact that gives meaning to our actions.

This pillar of Ikigai teaches us that true success is not measured solely by results but by our ability to use our skills to make a difference. Living in harmony with our vocation not only strengthens us in the face of challenges but also brings us closer to a life that is full, rewarding, and aligned with our deepest purpose.

What the World Needs (Mission)

The third pillar of Ikigai, what the world needs, represents the element of mission: the connection between what you do and the positive impact you can have on others and society. This aspect goes beyond merely satisfying your own interests or expressing your abilities, linking you to a broader, universal dimension. Mission is how your actions contribute to a greater good, generating value not just for yourself but for the world around you. Unlike passion, which focuses on what you love, and vocation, which is based on what you're good at, mission invites you to look beyond yourself. It asks you to consider the world's needs and challenges and reflect on how you can make a meaningful contribution. This doesn't mean you need to embark on an extraordinary path or tackle major global issues; often, mission is found in small, everyday actions that address real needs. For example, you might find your mission in supporting a social cause like education or mental health, or in protecting the environment through sustainable lifestyle choices. A volunteer dedicating their time to teaching valuable skills to an underserved community is addressing a concrete need. Similarly, an entrepreneur developing innovative solutions to reduce environmental impact is aligning with a mission that transcends personal profit. Mission thrives on empathy and awareness. It requires observing the world carefully and asking: "What are the needs around me? How can I use my talents and resources to make a difference?" This approach allows you to connect your personal purpose with a collective meaning, creating a sense of fulfillment that goes beyond individual boundaries.

Mission and Connection to Others

Mission not only adds depth to your life but also connects you to others in meaningful ways. It serves as the bridge between your Ikigai and the world, offering an opportunity to turn what you do into a contribution that leaves a positive mark, no matter how big or small.

The Meaning of "Mission"

Mission doesn't necessarily have to be tied to a singular, grand objective like solving climate change or combating social inequality (though it certainly can be). Rather, it refers to the sense of purpose you feel when your actions positively contribute to collective well-being. It's the idea that what you do has an impact, and that you're using your time, resources, and skills to meet a real need. This dimension of Ikigai not only adds meaning to your life but also connects you to people and the world on a deeper level. Whether it's helping a friend, supporting a community, or working on a project that improves others' lives, mission represents the driving force that motivates you to leave a positive mark.

Recognizing What the World Needs

Identifying what the world needs may seem like a complex task, but often the answers are right in front of us. Here are some questions to help guide your reflection:

- What issues resonate deeply with you?

- Consider the topics or causes you're passionate about: the environment, education, mental health, human rights, or others. These interests often point to areas where you can make a meaningful contribution.

- What needs do you see in your community?

Look around: are there unmet needs, gaps, or opportunities where your skills and abilities could make a difference? You may find that your contribution is closer than you think.

- How can you use what you love and what you're good at to help others?

Reflecting on your talents and passions can help you understand how to turn them into tools to meet the world's needs.

- What changes would you like to see in the world?

Sometimes, what the world needs aligns with the changes you want to see. Your mission might begin with a small action that, over time, inspires broader impact.

Balancing the Personal and the Collective

One of the main challenges of mission is finding a balance between what the world needs and what you can realistically offer. It's essential not to lose sight of your personal limits, avoiding the risk of overburdening yourself or feeling responsible for solving every global problem.

For example, a teacher passionate about education might choose to work in schools in disadvantaged areas to make a significant contribution. However, this decision could bring personal and emotional challenges, requiring careful balance between the mission's demands and their well-being. The key is to find sustainable ways to contribute without neglecting your own needs.

Examples of Missions in Daily Life

Mission doesn't have to be something grand or extraordinary; on the contrary, even small daily actions can have a significant impact on the lives of others and the world around us. Often, it's these simple but intentional acts that give meaning and purpose to our days.

Helping Others Through Your Work

Work is one of the primary contexts where we can express our mission. No matter your role, every profession offers opportunities to contribute to others' well-being.

For example, a doctor who approaches every patient with empathy is not only treating an illness but also building a human connection that provides comfort and reassurance. This approach not only enhances the patient's experience but also enriches the doctor's life, giving them a sense of truly making a difference.

Similarly, a craftsman who dedicates time and energy to creating high-quality objects contributes to improving the lives of the people who use their products. Whether it's a handmade piece of furniture, a carefully tailored garment, or a thoughtfully designed tool, these objects bring value and beauty to everyday life, embodying the idea of mission through well-done work.

Volunteering

Volunteering is one of the most immediate and tangible expressions of mission. Dedicating yourself to a cause you care about allows you to have a direct and concrete impact, whether it's helping people, animals, or the environment.

For example, a volunteer working at an animal shelter doesn't just provide food and care—they create a safe and loving environment for creatures that might otherwise suffer. Similarly, participating in social support initiatives, such as distributing meals to the homeless or spending time with the elderly, is a way to address real needs and build authentic connections. These small acts not only improve the lives of those involved but also strengthen the volunteer's sense of community and belonging.

Education and Sharing

Sharing values and knowledge is another powerful form of mission, often underestimated because it happens in everyday life. A parent teaching their children kindness, respect, and the importance of contributing to the collective good is not merely fulfilling a familial role—they are building the future. These values, passed on through example and dedication, can shape how the next generation interacts with the world and the people around them. Even outside the family context, sharing your skills and knowledge can be a meaningful mission. A teacher who spends extra time helping a struggling student or a professional mentoring younger colleagues contributes to a network of growth and support that extends beyond their immediate responsibilities.

Environmental Sustainability

One of the most relevant missions in modern society is protecting the planet. Adopting a sustainable lifestyle is not just a personal choice—it's a contribution to the collective well-being of current and future generations. Small daily actions, such as reducing plastic use, recycling correctly, or choosing eco-friendly transportation, can have a significant impact when adopted by a growing number of people.

For instance, choosing to buy local and seasonal products not only reduces the environmental impact of distribution chains but also supports local economies, creating a virtuous cycle. Similarly, sharing the importance of eco-friendly habits with friends and family can inspire others to make more conscious choices, multiplying the positive effect.

Conclusion

Mission doesn't require grand heroic acts; often, the smallest and most routine gestures can have a lasting impact. Whether helping others through your work, volunteering, educating and sharing values, or contributing to environmental sustainability, every intentional action can be a manifestation of mission.

What matters is acting with awareness, knowing that even the simplest choices can bring meaning and value to your life and to the lives of others. These examples show that mission can be integrated into many aspects of daily life. You don't have to change the world in a day—change often starts with small steps.

The Connection Between Mission and Happiness

Contributing to meeting a need in the world not only gives meaning to your life but can also enhance your happiness. Psychological studies show that helping others and feeling useful activates reward mechanisms in the brain, improving emotional well-being. When your work or actions address a real need, you experience a sense of fulfillment that goes beyond personal satisfaction. Additionally, living with a mission strengthens your sense of belonging and connection to others. You feel part of something larger, and this bond gives you strength even in difficult times. Knowing that your actions have a positive impact motivates you to keep going and continue to grow.

Conclusion

What the world needs is one of the most profound and meaningful pillars of Ikigai. Through mission, you find a sense of purpose that extends beyond personal benefit, contributing to collective well-being. No matter how small or large your contribution may be, what matters is the intention to make a difference and the awareness that every action, no matter how modest, can have an impact. Mission is not just an opportunity to change the world but also to grow as an individual. It is a journey that connects you to others, gives you strength, and brings you closer to a life filled with meaning and harmony. Start with what is within your reach, and let your mission grow with you, step by step.

What You Can Be Paid For (Profession)

The fourth pillar of Ikigai, what you can be paid for, represents the practical and sustainable aspect of your purpose in life. This element connects your passions and skills with the professional world, allowing you to build a career or business that not only aligns with your interests but also provides financial stability.

Finding a profession where you can express your abilities, contribute to what the world needs, and be adequately compensated is one of the keys to living in harmony with your Ikigai.

Profession as an Expression of Your Value

A profession is not just a way to earn a living—it can become an expression of your value and contribution to society. When you combine what you're good at, what you love, and what the world is willing to pay for, work transforms from a mere obligation into an opportunity to live with purpose and satisfaction.

For example, a designer with a talent for creativity might find professional fulfillment by designing innovative solutions to improve people's lives. Similarly, a consultant with strong analytical and communication skills might help businesses solve complex problems, earning financial rewards while making a positive impact.

The key is to find the intersection between what you excel at and what the market needs.

How to Find a Profession Aligned with Your Ikigai

Finding a profession that reflects your Ikigai can be challenging, but the process starts with a few essential questions:

- **What skills do you have that are in demand?**

- Evaluate the abilities you've developed over time and identify those that are useful in a professional context. For example, if you're skilled at problem-solving, consider careers in engineering, consulting, or project management.

- **What excites you, and how can you monetize it?**

If you have a passion, think about how to turn it into a profession. For example, someone passionate about photography could offer services for events, weddings, or create content for businesses.

- **What are the current needs of the job market?**

Observe market trends and areas where there's growing demand. Technology, sustainability, and healthcare are expanding sectors that offer many opportunities to align your purpose with financial rewards.

- **How can you differentiate yourself?**

In a competitive world, it's important to identify what makes you unique. This could be a combination of skills, a creative approach, or specialization in a specific field.

- **What skills do you have that are in demand?**

- Evaluate the abilities you've developed over time and identify those that are useful in a professional context. For example, if you're skilled at problem-solving, consider careers in engineering, consulting, or project management.

- **What excites you, and how can you monetize it?**

If you have a passion, think about how to turn it into a profession. For example, someone passionate about photography could offer services for events, weddings, or create content for businesses.

- **What are the current needs of the job market?**

Observe market trends and areas where there's growing demand. Technology, sustainability, and healthcare are expanding sectors that offer many opportunities to align your purpose with financial rewards.

- **How can you differentiate yourself?**

In a competitive world, it's important to identify what makes you unique. This could be a combination of skills, a creative approach, or specialization in a specific field.

The Importance of Economic Sustainability

A fundamental aspect of "what you can be paid for" is economic sustainability. While passion and mission are essential elements of your Ikigai, without a solid financial foundation, you may find yourself struggling. It's important to build a profession that not only fulfills you but also allows you to live comfortably, meeting your material needs and those of your family. This doesn't necessarily mean earning exorbitant amounts but finding a balance between doing what you love and achieving financial security. For example, a teacher passionate about education could supplement their income by offering private lessons or creating online courses. This approach not only strengthens financial stability but also expands their impact and sense of fulfillment.

Challenges and Opportunities in Finding the Right Profession

Finding a profession aligned with your Ikigai can come with challenges. Many people feel stuck in jobs they don't love or that don't value their skills. However, these situations can be seen as opportunities to reflect and redefine your path.

For instance, a dissatisfied employee might discover that their organizational skills could be used to start their own business, such as an event management or corporate consulting service. Similarly, a recent graduate struggling to find work in their field could explore opportunities in related areas or develop new skills through courses or hands-on experiences.

The key is to maintain an open and flexible mindset, seeking opportunities that align your purpose with market needs. Sometimes, this requires stepping out of your comfort zone, taking calculated risks, and investing time in your professional growth.

Integrating Profession Into Your Ikigai

When your profession is aligned with your Ikigai, you not only find a balance between work and personal life but also build a career that allows you to grow continuously. This doesn't mean every day will be free of challenges, but you'll feel that your work has purpose and that the time and energy you invest are well spent.

For example, a doctor choosing to work in a clinic serving underprivileged communities may find immense satisfaction in knowing they're improving the lives of those in need while maintaining financial stability. This approach integrates passion, mission, and vocation into a profession that enriches not only themselves but also those who benefit from their work.

Conclusion

"What you can be paid for" is an essential pillar of Ikigai because it connects your personal purpose with economic reality. Finding a profession that satisfies this aspect enables you to live with intention, build a meaningful career, and support yourself and your family.It's not just about income but about creating a balance between passion, vocation, and mission, turning work into a fundamental element of a life filled with meaning and fulfillment.

How These Elements Intertwine in Your Life

The four pillars of Ikigai—what you love, what you are good at, what the world needs, and what you can be paid for—are not separate compartments but interwoven elements that influence and strengthen each other. When you manage to integrate them harmoniously into your life, you create a deep sense of purpose that guides your daily decisions and allows you to live with intention and fulfillment. The intertwining of your internal world, represented by what you love and what you are good at, with the external world, encompassing what the world needs and what you can be paid for, happens when you find the balance between your personal interests, skills, and the demands of your environment. It is in this balance that your Ikigai resides: the ideal place where your passions and competencies transform into a meaningful contribution to the world while ensuring economic sustainability. Practical Examples of the Interplay Between Internal and External Worlds Imagine someone who loves teaching and has a talent for explaining complex concepts in a simple and engaging way. This person might find their Ikigai by becoming a teacher, mentor, or trainer. Through teaching, they not only transmit knowledge but inspire, guide, and positively influence their students' lives, creating a lasting impact. Another example could be someone passionate about environmental sustainability and skilled in marketing. They could identify a growing market need, such as the transition to a greener economy, and use their communication and promotion skills to build a career in renewable energy or collaborate with companies developing sustainable solutions. The result would be twofold: contributing to a pressing global need, such as combating climate change, while creating a meaningful and financially rewarding profession.

Key Questions to Explore Your Ikigai

To find your Ikigai, reflect on these key questions:

1. **What do I love and excel at?**

Identify the activities that excite you and where you naturally have talent.

2. **What are the current needs of the world around me?**

Reflect on global or local problems that interest you and consider how you could contribute.

3. **How can I combine these elements to create value?**

Think about how your passions and skills can translate into solutions with a tangible impact.

The Process of Finding Balance

The interplay between these elements doesn't always happen linearly or immediately. You might need to explore different opportunities or experiment with various roles before finding the right balance. For example, someone with a passion for writing and technical skills might start as a copywriter for tech companies, only to discover their true Ikigai lies in creating educational content about sustainability.

This process takes time, but every step brings you closer to a deeper connection between your internal and external worlds.

The Heart of Ikigai: Balancing the Internal and External

To understand how the four pillars intertwine, recognize that two of them—what you love and what you are good at—reflect your internal world. They represent your passions, talents, and personal identity. The other two pillars—what the world needs and what you can be paid for—refer to the external world, including societal opportunities and needs. The connection occurs when you link these two worlds. For example:

- A person who loves teaching (internal world) and is skilled at explaining complex ideas might find their Ikigai by becoming a teacher or mentor (connection with the external world).

- Similarly, someone passionate about environmental sustainability and skilled in marketing might build a career in renewable energy, addressing a global need while earning a living.

The Dynamic Between Passion and Vocation

Passion (what you love) and vocation (what you are good at) are often the starting points for discovering your Ikigai. However, these two dimensions alone are not enough to create a fully satisfying life.

You can love something and have talent in a particular field, but without finding a way to apply it to a real need or make a living from it, you might feel frustrated or unfulfilled.

- For instance, a talented musician may have a deep love for music, but without a strategy to turn that passion into a sustainable career, they might face financial difficulties.

- Similarly, someone passionate about writing might feel dissatisfied if they don't see how their work improves others' lives or addresses a demand in the publishing market.

Conclusion

The intertwining of these elements is not a destination but a continuous process of discovery and growth. Finding this balance requires flexibility and openness to change, as your passions and skills evolve over time, just as the world's needs do. Staying aware of these dynamics allows you to adapt and create a life that remains meaningful and fulfilling at every stage.

The Connection Between Mission and Profession

Mission (what the world needs) and profession (what you can be paid for) represent the bridge between your personal desires and the social and economic context. When you find a way to align what you do with a real need, you create value not only for yourself but also for others. This connection is crucial for building an Ikigai that is not only fulfilling but also sustainable in the long term.

For instance, an entrepreneur passionate about technology and skilled in programming might identify a gap in the market, such as the need for digital solutions to improve access to healthcare services. By starting a business that addresses this need, the entrepreneur creates not only a lucrative profession but also contributes to enhancing people's quality of life.

When the Pillars Are Out of Balance

The four pillars of Ikigai—what you love, what you are good at, what the world needs, and what you can be paid for—are not always perfectly balanced in our lives. It's common, and entirely normal, to go through periods where one or more of these elements are misaligned. However, these disconnections should not be seen as failures but as opportunities to reflect, reevaluate your priorities, and make gradual adjustments.

For example:

- **Unfulfilling Work:** You might be in a job that provides financial security but doesn't excite you or utilize your true skills. This can lead to frustration or demotivation, particularly if the work lacks purpose or meaning.

- **Passion Without Sustainability:** You may be deeply passionate about an activity, such as art, music, or writing, but struggle to turn it into a sustainable career. This situation can be disheartening, as you balance doing what you love with meeting your financial needs.

- **Skills Without Demand:** You may have exceptional expertise in a field, but discover that your skills no longer meet a real-world need. For instance, being an expert in obsolete technology could make it difficult to find opportunities in today's market, leading to feelings of irrelevance.

Addressing Disconnections: A Practical Guide

When the pillars of your Ikigai are out of balance, it's important to recognize this and take steps to restore harmony.

1. **Reflect on Your Current Priorities**

Ask yourself which of the four pillars feels most distant or underdeveloped in your life. Are you satisfied with what you do but feel it lacks meaning? Or do you love what you do but struggle to earn a living? Identifying the area of imbalance is the first step toward addressing it.

2. **Experiment with Small Changes**

You don't need to overhaul your life overnight. Start with small changes that help integrate the missing pillars. For example, if your job isn't aligned with what you love, dedicate time to side projects that excite you, such as volunteering or pursuing a hobby. This allows you to nurture your passion without giving up financial security

Invest in Personal Development

If you feel your skills are outdated or lack the expertise to align the pillars, consider investing in yourself. Take a course, acquire a new skill, or explore an area that interests you. This not only helps you feel more prepared but also opens up new professional and personal opportunities. Cultivate a Long-Term Vision When the pillars are unbalanced, it's easy to feel stuck or overwhelmed. Remember that Ikigai is a journey, not a destination. Focus on what you can do in the short term to move closer to your ideal balance while maintaining a clear vision of your long-term goals.

Concrete Examples of Adjustments

- **A Teacher Seeking More Flexibility**: A teacher who loves educating but feels trapped in a rigid school system could explore alternatives like private tutoring or creating online courses on topics they are passionate about. This allows them to continue doing what they love in a more flexible and creative environment.
- **A Struggling Creative Professional**: A graphic designer or photographer struggling to find clients might reflect on how their skills can better meet market needs. They could specialize in a niche area, such as branding for sustainable small businesses, creating a connection between their work and what the world needs
- **Accepting and Valuing the Process**

It is essential to accept that imbalance between the pillars is part of the journey. Each phase of life offers new opportunities to realign your goals and priorities. Disconnections, while uncomfortable, represent moments of growth that push you to explore new paths and discover creative solutions. The key is to maintain flexibility and curiosity, using these moments as opportunities to move closer to your Ikigai. When you learn to see these challenges as an integral part of your path, you begin to build a life that is not perfect but truly reflects who you are and what you want to offer the world.

Integrating the Pillars Into Daily Life

Integrating the four pillars of Ikigai into your life does not necessarily require drastic changes or personal revolutions. Often, the process begins with small steps and a greater awareness of the connections that already exist between your daily actions and your deeper values.

It's about recognizing the potential of what you already do every day and finding ways to align your activities with what you love, what you are good at, what the world needs, and what you can be paid for. Here are some practical strategies to make Ikigai a part of your everyday life:

Reflect on Your Daily Activities

Take time to analyze your routine and ask how your current activities connect to the four pillars. For example:

- Does your work utilize your skills and allow you to express what you love doing?

- Do your daily actions address a real need, whether in your community or the world?
- Do you find satisfaction in what you do, or are there areas you'd like to explore more deeply?

For instance, if you work as a project manager but love writing, consider how to integrate writing into your day—perhaps by maintaining a personal blog or contributing to corporate content that reflects your voice

Seek Opportunities for Alignment

If your main job or activities don't fulfill all the pillars, explore ways to incorporate your passions through side projects or extracurricular activities. For example: • If you're an engineer who loves cooking, consider organizing dinners for friends or community events on weekends.

- If you work in an office but are passionate about the environment, propose workplace sustainability initiatives, like recycling programs or awareness cam-paigns.

These activities not only enrich your personal life but can also open new professional and social doors.

- If you're an engineer who loves cooking, consider organizing dinners for friends or community events on weekends.
- If you work in an office but are passionate about the environment, propose workplace sustainability initiatives, like recycling programs or awareness

campaigns.

These activities not only enrich your personal life but can also open new professional and social doors.

Commit to Personal Growth

Investing in developing your skills is an effective way to expand your opportunities and bring yourself closer to your Ikigai. For example:

- Enroll in courses to improve abilities like communication, leadership, or a technical skill you want to refine.

- Use your free time to study, practice, or engage in what excites you and can enhance your career or societal contribution.

Examples:

- An **administrative worker** passionate about organization might learn advanced project management tools or spreadsheet techniques to enhance their efficiency and find greater satisfaction in bringing order to daily activities.

- A **sales associate** passionate about interpersonal relationships might take communication or advanced sales courses to better interact with customers and open new career opportunities, such as sales management or customer care.

- A **driver** interested in technology might learn to use logistics apps or route-planning platforms, gaining skills that could lead to specialized roles like fleet management or corporate logistics.

These examples show that even seemingly common jobs offer opportunities for growth, turning daily activities into sources of satisfaction and career possibilities. The key is to invest time and effort to integrate your passions and skills into your professional context.

Find Meaning in Small Gestures

Ikigai isn't only found in grand achievements but also in everyday gestures. Every action can reflect your purpose if done with intention:

- Offer to help a struggling colleague, fostering a more collaborative work environment.

- Dedicate time to a local cause, such as volunteering at a soup kitchen or cleaning a park.

These simple acts can have a positive impact not only on others but also on yourself, providing a sense of connection and meaning.

Conclusion

The four pillars of Ikigai intertwine in your life like the threads of a tapestry, creating a complete picture of who you are and what you can offer the world. This interweaving is not static—it evolves over time, shaped by your experiences and the changes in the world around you. The key is to keep an open mind and a heart willing to explore new possibilities. When you manage to balance what you love, what you are good at, what the world needs, and what you can be paid for, you create a life that is not only meaningful but also sustainable and fulfilling. This is the heart of Ikigai: finding harmony between your personal desires and your contribution to the world.

Chapter 3
The Benefits of Ikigai

"True happiness is when we stop searching for it outside and begin to cultivate it within ourselves."

— Dilgo Khyentse Rinpoche —

Inner Harmony: Living in Balance with Oneself

One of the primary benefits of Ikigai is its ability to cultivate a sense of inner harmony, which translates into a deep balance within oneself. This state of serenity doesn't mean living without problems or challenges but rather facing life with emotional and mental stability, enabling you to navigate difficulties without feeling overwhelmed. Living in balance with oneself is fundamental for leading an authentic and meaningful life, and Ikigai helps us achieve just that.

What Is Inner Harmony?

Inner harmony is a state of balance between the different dimensions of our being: mind, body, and spirit. It means being at peace with who we are, accepting our imperfections, and continually working to improve without judging ourselves too harshly. Ikigai invites us to explore our life's purpose by uniting what we love to do, our skills, the world's needs, and economic opportunities. This process helps us live in alignment with our values and most authentic desires, promoting a sense of coherence between who we are and what we do.

The Role of Self-Awareness

The journey to inner harmony begins with self-awareness. Ikigai encourages us to reflect on what truly matters to us, to explore our passions, strengths, and aspirations. When we take the time to know ourselves better, we can identify the internal conflicts that often throw us off balance—unrealistic expectations, external pressures, or comparisons with others.

For example, many people live under the weight of societal standards, such as financial success or physical perfection, forgetting what genuinely makes them happy. Ikigai helps free us from these influences, encouraging us to find our own personal rhythm. Living in harmony means recognizing that our value doesn't depend on others' expectations but on our connection to our purpose.

Cultivating Balance in Everyday Life

Inner harmony is not a state you achieve once and for all; it's a process that requires constant effort. Here are some daily practices inspired by Ikigai to help maintain this balance:

1. **Practice Gratitude**

Gratitude is one of the most powerful practices for living in harmony with oneself. It involves recognizing and appreciating the simple yet meaningful things we often take for granted, like a warm meal, a sunny day, or a heartfelt conversation with a friend. Gratitude shifts our focus from lack to abundance, reducing stress and fostering a positive mindset.

a. To make this practice more concrete, try writing down three things you're grateful for each day. This simple exercise helps you live in the present and cultivate greater awareness of the blessings already present in your life.

2. **Take Care of Your Body**

Your body is the temple where you live, and keeping it healthy is essential for feeling balanced. Ikigai emphasizes the importance of a healthy lifestyle, which includes balanced nutrition, regular exercise, and adequate rest. A healthy body supports a healthy mind, promoting emotional and mental resilience.

a. Start your day with a nutritious breakfast, such as fresh fruit and whole grains.

b. Incorporate physical activity into your routine, even just a 20-minute walk or a short yoga session.

c. Establish a sleep routine that allows for 7-8 hours of rest each night, creating a calm and relaxing environment for sleeping.

3. **Create an Intentional Routine**

A well-structured and intentional routine can reduce anxiety and increase your sense of control over your day. Plan activities that reflect your values and goals, dedicating time each day to what you're passionate about.

a. For example, if you love writing, reserve 30 minutes every morning to work on a personal project.

b.   If meditation helps you relax, include it in your evening routine. Creating space for what brings you joy and meaning not only boosts productivity but also helps you live with greater awareness and intentionality.

4.   Reflect on Your Progress

Reflection is a fundamental tool for maintaining inner balance and monitoring your journey toward Ikigai. Take a few minutes at the end of each day to write in a journal or simply reflect mentally on your actions. Ask questions like:

a.   "What successes did I achieve today?"

b.   "What could I have done better?"

c.   "How did I feel about my actions today?"

This exercise helps you acknowledge your progress, learn from your mistakes, and stay aligned with your goals. Over time, this practice provides greater clarity about your path and strengthens your connection to your Ikigai.

Daily Practices for Inner Harmony

These daily practices, when integrated consistently, allow you to live in balance, cultivate your inner harmony, and face life's challenges with greater serenity

The Connection Between Ikigai and Resilience

Inner harmony also makes us more resilient, enabling us to face life's challenges without losing our balance. When we know our purpose and live in alignment with it, we are less likely to be overwhelmed by stress or adversity.

Ikigai gives us a compass—a direction to guide us even in times of crisis.

For example, someone who has found their Ikigai in caring for others, such as a doctor or teacher, can approach the challenges of their profession with greater serenity, knowing that what they do is meaningful. This awareness provides strength and motivation, even in the face of difficult obstacles.

Inner Harmony and Relationships

Another essential aspect of inner harmony is its impact on relationships. When we are balanced within ourselves, we are more open and available to others. Our interactions become more authentic because we are not driven by the need for approval or the fear of being judged. Ikigai helps us build relationships based on shared values, creating a sense of connection that enriches both us and those around us.For instance, someone who lives in harmony with their Ikigai might become a point of reference for their community, offering support and inspiration to others seeking their own purpose. This not only strengthens social bonds but also contributes to emotional well-being.

The Journey Toward Inner Harmony

Finding inner harmony is a journey, not a destination. It requires patience, dedication, and openness to change. There will be moments when you feel off balance, but it is precisely in these times that Ikigai can serve as a valuable guide. Whenever you drift away from your center, use the four pillars as a reference point to recalibrate your path.

Inner harmony doesn't mean living without problems but rather facing life with a solid foundation of awareness, acceptance, and intentionality. It is the result of a deep alignment between who you are, what you do, and what you desire. When you cultivate this harmony, you not only live better but also face challenges with strength and serenity, contributing to the world in meaningful ways.

Ikigai is not just a tool for finding purpose but also a philosophy for living with balance and inner peace.

Cultivating this harmony allows you to build a life that reflects your values, dreams, and desire to contribute to the collective good.

Happiness and Satisfaction: Finding Joy in Small Things

Happiness is not necessarily tied to grand achievements or extraordinary goals. One of the fundamental principles of Ikigai is that true satisfaction lies in the ability to appreciate life's small, everyday pleasures. This mindset enables us to live fully and with gratitude, finding joy even in the simplest and most ordinary moments. Ikigai teaches us that the secret to happiness lies in living mindfully, cultivating presence, and recognizing the intrinsic value of daily experiences.

The Japanese Concept of "Ikigai-kan"

In Japanese culture, the term Ikigai-kan describes the sense of fulfillment and serenity that comes from living according to one's purpose. This state is not achieved through material successes but through the ability to find meaning in the small actions of daily life.

For instance, a morning walk in nature, the taste of a good cup of tea, or the smile of a loved one can become sources of deep happiness.

The kan (feeling) associated with Ikigai is an invitation to slow down, live in the present moment, and appreciate what often goes unnoticed. The idea is not to ignore life's problems or challenges but to balance them with the joy that comes from simple, authentic experiences.

The Connection Between Simplicity and Happiness

One of the most valuable teachings of Ikigai is that happiness does not require complications. In an increasingly fast-paced world where we are constantly bombarded with messages urging us to want more—more money, more success, more material goods—Ikigai reminds us that true fulfillment comes from simplicity. It is a philosophy that encourages us to look beyond superficial desires and rediscover the value of daily experiences.

For instance, an elderly resident of Okinawa, one of Japan's regions with the highest rates of longevity and well-being, might find happiness in tending to their garden or preparing a meal for loved ones. These actions are neither grand nor extraordinary but represent moments of connection with oneself and the surrounding world.

This perspective is equally applicable to modern life. Finding joy in small things means rediscovering the pleasure of a captivating book, an honest conversation, or an unhurried sunset. Happiness is not far away; it is often all around us, ready to be noticed.

The Role of Gratitude in Daily Satisfaction

A key element in finding joy in small things is the practice of gratitude. Being grateful does not mean ignoring difficulties but learning to see the positive side even in the most common situations. Ikigai encourages us to begin each day with an appreciative mindset: being thankful for the food we eat, the people in our lives, or the opportunities we are given.

A practical way to cultivate gratitude is by keeping a journal where, every evening, you write down three things that brought you happiness during the day.

These moments could be small, like the aroma of morning coffee, or more significant, like the support of a friend during a tough time. This habit helps shift the focus from lack to abundance, enhancing your emotional and mental well-being.

The Importance of "Here and Now"

Another central aspect of finding joy in small things is living in the present moment. Often, our minds are occupied with worries about the future or regrets about the past, preventing us from appreciating what is happening right now. Ikigai invites us to focus on the "here and now," embracing each moment with openness and curiosity. For example, the next time you drink a cup of tea, try doing it intentionally: observe the color of the beverage, feel the warmth in your hands, and savor each sip. This approach, akin to mindfulness practice, helps you live more consciously and find pleasure even in the simplest acts

Shared Happiness: The Power of Relationships

Joy is not just an individual experience; it often amplifies when shared. Human relationships play a fundamental role in our daily satisfaction, and Ikigai emphasizes the importance of building meaningful connections.

Sharing a meal, laughing together, or simply spending time with loved ones are moments that enrich our lives.

Even small acts of kindness toward others can bring happiness. A smile, a sincere compliment, or offering help without expectations not only improves the recipient's day but also strengthens our sense of connection to the world.

Incorporating Ikigai into Your Daily Life

Finding joy in small things requires intentionality and conscious effort. Happiness cannot be left to chance; we must actively create it.

A good starting point is carving out a moment each day to reflect on what brings you pleasure or satisfaction. For example, take five minutes in the morning to think about something positive awaiting you during the day, like a coffee break with a colleague or time spent reading a book you love. Dedicate time to activities that excite you, even if they are small. If you love music, set aside time to play an instrument or listen to your favorite songs. If cooking brings you joy, try a new recipe or cook for someone you care about. These moments not only bring happiness but also help you connect with yourself and your deepest values. Surround yourself with people who uplift you and share your vision of life. Even a brief meeting with an honest friend or a phone call with a family member can enrich your day. Authentic relationships are a source of energy and happiness, and Ikigai encourages you to cultivate them attentively. In difficult times, Ikigai helps you see beyond immediate challenges. Always seek a ray of light: a small personal victory, a kind gesture received, or a lesson learned from a mistake. This approach allows you to maintain a positive perspective and build a life rooted in meaning, even when things feel complicated. The key is learning to recognize the value in every moment, big or small.

Conclusion

Happiness and satisfaction are not necessarily found in major accomplishments but in the ability to appreciate the small things that make up our everyday lives. Ikigai teaches us to slow down, live with gratitude, and discover joy in the details that often go unnoticed. Cultivating this mindset will allow you to navigate life with a light heart and an open mind, building a life rooted in well-being and fulfillment.

Longevity and Well-being: The Secret of Okinawa's Inhabitants

Okinawa, a Japanese archipelago located in the southern part of the country, is renowned worldwide for its remarkable number of centenarians. This region is one of the so-called Blue Zones—geographic areas where people live longer and enjoy an extraordinarily high quality of life. But what is the secret to this longevity? Many researchers agree that one of the key factors is Ikigai, a life philosophy deeply ingrained in the local culture, combining purpose, social connection, and a healthy lifestyle.

The Connection Between Ikigai and Longevity

The people of Okinawa attribute much of their longevity to living according to their Ikigai. This concept, which translates to "reason for being" or "reason to wake up in the morning," is not just an abstract idea but a tangible practice that guides their daily lives. Individuals with a clear Ikigai approach life with optimism and resilience—traits that have positive effects on both physical and mental health. Scientific studies have shown that having a purpose in life is associated with lower levels of stress, blood pressure, and inflammation—three critical factors in preventing chronic diseases and promoting longevity. For instance, many Okinawans continue to engage in meaningful activities well into old age. A farmer may keep tending to their garden, while a craftsman might work passionately on their projects. This sense of utility and contribution to the community not only enhances their mental health but also bolsters their physical well-being.

A Balanced Lifestyle

Another key factor in Okinawa's longevity is their balanced lifestyle, which integrates diet, movement, social connections, and healthy daily habits. Ikigai does not exist in isolation—it is closely tied to these practices, which work together to create a harmonious and sustainable way of living.

Balanced Diet and Moderation

The traditional Okinawan diet is rich in vegetables, tofu, seaweed, fish, and small amounts of lean meat. Central to their dietary habits is the concept of hara hachi bu, a principle that encourages eating until one is 80% full, avoiding overindulgence. This moderation not only helps maintain a healthy weight but also reduces the risk of metabolic diseases such as diabetes and cardiovascular illnesses.

Natural and Consistent Physical Activity

Okinawans don't frequent gyms but incorporate movement naturally into their daily routines. Whether it's walking, working in the fields, or engaging in traditional arts such as dance or pottery, physical activity is seen as an integral part of life rather than an obligation. This approach helps maintain a strong and agile body, even in old age.

Meaningful Relationships

Community plays a fundamental role in the lives of Okinawans. They belong to social groups called moai, small circles of friends who provide mutual emotional, social, and even financial support. This sense of belonging and connection reduces feelings of isolation, improves mental health, and contributes to greater emotional resilience.

Rituals and Gratitude

Okinawan culture emphasizes the value of daily rituals, which may include moments of reflection, prayer, or simple appreciation for the beauty of nature. Practicing gratitude is a central element of their life philosophy, helping them maintain a positive outlook even in the face of challenges.

The Mind-Body Connection

Ikigai doesn't just influence the mindset of Okinawans; it has a direct impact on their physical health. Studies have shown that people who live with purpose have lower cortisol levels—the stress hormone—and stronger immune systems. This is especially important in old age, when the body becomes more vulnerable to illnesses. For example, an elderly Okinawan woman who finds joy in tending her garden not only keeps her body active but also experiences a sense of peace and satisfaction that supports her mental health. This balance between mind and body is one of the primary reasons many Okinawans live to 100 with an extraordinary quality of life.

Lessons from Ikigai for the Modern World

What can we learn from the people of Okinawa? Even if we don't live in a Blue Zone like Okinawa, we can draw inspiration from their principles to improve our well-being and enrich our quality of life. The people of Okinawa demonstrate that small changes and daily habits can have a profound impact on physical, mental, and emotional balance. Here are some ways to integrate their teachings into our lives.

Find a Meaningful Activity

Dedicate time to an activity that brings you satisfaction and a sense of purpose. It could be something you're passionate about, like caring for plants, experimenting with creative recipes, or working on a craft project. For instance, if you love writing, you might start a blog or keep a journal to express your ideas.

Another option could be participating in initiatives that allow you to contribute to your neighborhood, such as helping with a local goods drive. Integrating meaningful activities into your routine not only helps reduce stress but also provides a sense of personal accomplishment.

Cultivate Authentic Relationships

The people of Okinawa place great value on social connections, as exemplified by their moai, small support groups that serve as social and moral networks.

You can also strengthen your relationships by spending quality time with friends and family. Organize a game night, share a carefully prepared meal, or simply enjoy a heartfelt conversation with a loved one. These moments of connection enhance your emotional well-being, helping you feel part of something greater.

Eat in Moderation: The Principle of Hara Hachi Bu

One of the secrets of Okinawa's inhabitants is the concept of hara hachi bu, which means stopping eating when you're 80% full. This practice not only helps avoid excess calorie intake but also promotes healthy digestion and reduces the risk of chronic illnesses. To adopt this habit, try eating slowly and choosing simple, nutritious foods, such as seasonal vegetables, fresh fish, legumes, and whole grains. For example, you can prepare balanced meals like a bowl of miso soup with vegetables, paired with brown rice and a portion of tofu or fish. Eating mindfully allows you to listen to your body and fully savor the flavors of your meal

Find Moments of Stillness

A key aspect of Okinawa's lifestyle is the ability to carve out moments of stillness to reflect and connect with oneself. Even amidst the busyness of modern life, you can find time to pause, practice gratitude, or relax.

For instance, you might start your day by meditating for five minutes, taking a peaceful walk in a park, or writing down a positive thought about what makes you happy. Simple activities like watching a sunset or listening to calming music can also help you restore a sense of calm and awareness.

Incorporating Okinawa's Principles into Modern Life

Incorporating the principles of Okinawa's inhabitants into your life doesn't require major changes—just small adjustments to your daily routine. Finding activities that bring you joy, building authentic relationships, eating in moderation, and dedicating time to stillness are simple but powerful steps to enhance your physical and mental well-being. By following these teachings, you can enrich your life and move closer to a more balanced and fulfilling version of yourself.

Conclusion

The longevity and well-being of Okinawa's inhabitants are not the result of a single factor but of a balance between a clear purpose, a healthy lifestyle, and a strong connection to the community. Ikigai is the thread that ties these elements together, offering a guide to living a long, meaningful, and fulfilling life. By incorporating even a few of these principles into your daily routine, you can improve your physical and emotional well-being, bringing you closer to your personal Ikigai.

Stories of People Who Embody Ikigai

Ikigai is not merely an abstract philosophical concept but a practical guide that manifests in the real lives of many people. In Japan, this approach to life is authentically and personally experienced, influencing the country's culture and lifestyle. The stories of those who embody Ikigai offer inspiration and insight into how we can find balance, meaning, and happiness in our daily lives. Here are some testimonials that demonstrate how Ikigai can transform lives.

The Wisdom of Longevity: Haru, the Farmer from Okinawa

Haru, a 94-year-old man living in a small village on the island of Okinawa, is a vivid example of how Ikigai can positively influence longevity and well-being. Every day, Haru wakes up early to tend to his garden, a passion he has cultivated for decades. Working the land is not just a way to stay physically active but also a way to feel connected to nature and his community. Haru regularly shares his fresh produce with neighbors, finding satisfaction in knowing that what he grows contributes to others' well-being. For Haru, the garden is more than just a physical activity—it is a way to live with purpose. As Haru often says, "Every seed I plant is a reminder that I'm contributing to something greater than myself." This connection to nature, community, and a sense of daily utility lies at the heart of his Ikigai.

Mastery of Traditional Art: Keiko, the Ceramicist

Keiko, a ceramicist from Kyoto, embodies Ikigai through her dedication to traditional Japanese art. For over forty years, she has perfected the technique of raku, a form of pottery that requires patience, precision, and a deep connection to the creative process. Keiko does not see pottery as merely a craft but as a means of self-expression and a way to keep alive a tradition that dates back centuries.

Each piece she creates is unique and imperfect, reflecting the Japanese principle of wabi-sabi, which celebrates the beauty of imperfection. For Keiko, Ikigai lies in the combination of creativity, commitment, and connection to the history of her art. "Every time I hold clay in my hands, I feel part of a flow that goes beyond myself," she explains. Her work not only provides her with a sense of purpose but also inspires those who admire her creations, proving that Ikigai can be found in the act of creating.

A Sense of Belonging: Hiroshi, the Fisherman from Hokkaido

Hiroshi, a 62-year-old fisherman living along the coast of Hokkaido, represents another example of Ikigai embodied in daily life. His day begins before dawn, as he prepares to head out to sea in his small boat. For Hiroshi, fishing is not just a job but a tradition passed down through generations in his family.

Despite the challenges of the sea and the economic changes that have made fishing less profitable, Hiroshi finds his Ikigai in his connection to the ocean and the knowledge that he is contributing to his local community. The fish he catches are sold at local markets, providing food for families and restaurants in the area. "Every day I spend at sea reminds me of who I am and where I come from," says Hiroshi. His life is a testament to how Ikigai can be rooted in a sense of belonging and loyalty to one's roots.

Caring for Others: Emi, the Pediatric Nurse

Emi, a pediatric nurse in Tokyo, lives her Ikigai in her daily work caring for sick children and their families. Although her job is often demanding and stressful, Emi finds deep fulfillment in knowing that her efforts make a difference in people's lives.

For her, every smile from a recovered child or word of gratitude from a parent represents a moment of meaning in her profession. "There are difficult days, but remembering why I do this work gives me the strength to keep going," Emi says. Her Ikigai lies not only in her professional skills but also in her ability to offer comfort and hope during challenging times. Emi exemplifies how Ikigai can be found in serving others and building emotional connections.

Teaching the Next Generation: Takeshi, the Calligraphy Master

Takeshi, a calligraphy master in Tokyo, has devoted his life to teaching this traditional art to students of all ages. For him, calligraphy is not just a technique but a way to impart values such as discipline, focus, and inner harmony. Each class he teaches is an opportunity to inspire students to discover their creative potential.

"I don't just teach them how to write characters, but how to see the beauty in details and find balance in their lives," says Takeshi. His Ikigai is reflected in passing down cultural heritage to the next generation, ensuring that this ancient art continues to thrive. His example shows how Ikigai can be rooted in sharing knowledge and inspiring others.

Conclusion

The stories of Haru, Keiko, Hiroshi, Emi, and Takeshi demonstrate that Ikigai can be found in many different areas—from creativity to tradition, from serving others to connecting with nature. These examples remind us that living according to our Ikigai does not necessarily mean pursuing grand endeavors but finding meaning in daily actions and authentic connections. Each of these stories offers a universal lesson: the true purpose of life is to live in harmony with who we are, what we love, and the contribution we can make to the world

Connections with Other Japanese Philosophies: Wabi-Sabi, Zen, Kaizen

While Ikigai is a unique philosophy, it does not exist in isolation within Japanese culture. It intertwines deeply with other philosophical and cultural traditions that share complementary principles. Among these, Wabi-Sabi, Zen, and Kaizen are particularly significant, offering perspectives that enrich and complete our understanding of Ikigai. Exploring these connections allows us to grasp the depth and complexity of a worldview that celebrates balance, personal growth, and harmony with the world.

Wabi-Sabi: The Beauty of Imperfection

Wabi-Sabi is a Japanese philosophy that celebrates the beauty of imperfection, transience, and simplicity. It encourages us to find value in things that are imperfect, incomplete, or ephemeral, promoting an attitude of acceptance and gratitude for reality as it is. Ikigai, with its invitation to live authentically and with purpose, intertwines deeply with Wabi-Sabi. For example, Wabi-Sabi teaches us to see beauty in a ceramic cup with a small crack, interpreting it as a sign of the passage of time and the object's story. Similarly, Ikigai encourages us to recognize the value of our uniqueness, including the imperfections that make us human. We don't need to be perfect to live meaningfully; instead, embracing our imperfect nature allows us to live more authentically.In daily life, integrating Wabi-Sabi and Ikigai means accepting that our personal journeys will not be linear or obstacle-free. This approach encourages us to find joy in small moments, even during challenging circumstances, appreciating the journey rather than chasing an unattainable perfection.

Zen: Presence in the Moment

The philosophy of Zen, a branch of Buddhism deeply rooted in Japanese culture, focuses on the art of presence and connection with the present moment. Through practices such as meditation and mindfulness, Zen teaches us to live with simplicity and intentionality. This perspective aligns closely with Ikigai, which invites us to cultivate a sense of purpose through mindful and meaningful actions.

For instance, Zen emphasizes the importance of being fully present in every activity, whether it's drinking a cup of tea or tending a garden. This same focus on the present moment is central to Ikigai, urging us to live intentionally and appreciate each moment as part of our purpose. A crucial aspect of Zen is the practice of zazen (seated meditation), which helps calm the mind and develop greater awareness. For those following Ikigai, these practices can be invaluable tools for reconnecting with oneself and focusing on what truly matters. For example, a simple daily pause to take deep breaths or reflect can turn a hectic day into an opportunity to restore balance.

Kaizen: Continuous Improvement

Kaizen, a philosophy that translates literally to "change for the better," is based on the idea of continuous improvement through small steps. Originally developed as a methodology in the Japanese industrial context, Kaizen has become a principle applicable to all areas of personal and professional life. The connection with Ikigai is clear: both promote a gradual and intentional approach to building a meaningful life. Ikigai encourages living with purpose and authenticity, and Kaizen offers a practical method to achieve this. For example, if your Ikigai lies in writing, Kaizen suggests starting by dedicating just a few minutes a day to this activity, gradually increasing the time and continuously improving your skills. This approach removes the pressure of making large changes all at once, making it easier to achieve your goals. Another key aspect of Kaizen is ongoing reflection. Similarly, Ikigai invites us to regularly reevaluate our purpose, adapting it to evolving circumstances. This mindset of continuous improvement helps maintain balance and live a life rich in meaning without falling into complacency or stagnation.

The Synergies Between Ikigai, Wabi-Sabi, Zen, and Kaizen

These philosophies, while distinct, complement one another and enrich our understanding of Ikigai.

- Wabi-Sabi teaches us to accept imperfection and find beauty in simplicity.

- Zen encourages us to be fully present and mindful in the moment.

- Kaizen provides a practical framework for pursuing our purpose through continuous improvement.

For example, imagine a person whose Ikigai is cooking for others. Wabi-Sabi would encourage them to enjoy the process, even if the result isn't perfect. Zen would guide them to focus on every step of the preparation, from chopping ingredients to plating the dish. Kaizen, finally, would motivate them to gradually refine their recipes and techniques, transforming cooking into an ever-evolving art form.

Applying These Philosophies to Daily Life

Integrating Ikigai, Wabi-Sabi, Zen, and Kaizen into daily life can transform how we approach challenges, relationships, and aspirations.

Wabi-Sabi: Embracing Imperfection

Wabi-Sabi invites us to embrace imperfection as a natural part of life. Instead of viewing mistakes or failures as obstacles, we can see them as opportunities to grow and improve.

For instance, if a work project doesn't go as planned, rather than feeling discouraged, you can reflect on what you've learned and how these lessons can guide you in the future. Similarly, accepting imperfection in personal relationships—such as misunderstandings or disagreements—allows you to approach them with more compassion, strengthening bonds. This philosophy encourages you to see beauty in what is authentic and unique, including your own personal experience.

Zen: Living in the Present Moment

Zen teaches us to be fully present in every moment, approaching daily activities with mindfulness and intention. For example, while drinking a cup of tea, you can focus on the warmth of the cup, the aroma of the beverage, and the taste of each sip.

This approach doesn't require radical changes but small moments of attention that transform ordinary actions into meaningful experiences. The practice of meditation, even for just five minutes a day, is a powerful tool to calm the mind and restore focus.

Kaizen: Continuous Improvement

Kaizen encourages you to identify an area of your life you'd like to improve and adopt small daily changes to make progress.

For example, if you want to improve your physical fitness, you could start with a 10-minute walk each day, gradually increasing the time and intensity. The same principle can be applied to work, time management, or nurturing relationships. This approach allows you to achieve big goals through simple, consistent steps, avoiding overwhelm and maintaining motivation.

Conclusion

Ikigai, enriched by the philosophies of Wabi-Sabi, Zen, and Kaizen, offers a complete and harmonious vision of life. Together, these traditions teach us to live with awareness, acceptance, and a continuous commitment to personal growth. Applying them in our daily lives allows us to build a life that not only reflects our purposes and values but also connects us to beauty, presence, and continuous progress.

Ikigai and Social Connections: The Value of Belonging

One of the central aspects of Ikigai is the bond it creates with others. While Ikigai is often seen as a personal journey to discover one's purpose, in Japan, it is deeply tied to relationships and a sense of social inclusion. Human connections and the feeling of being part of something larger are fundamental to finding meaning in life, especially during challenging times

The Importance of Social Bonds in Japanese Culture

In Japan, connections between individuals are valued and carefully nurtured. One of the most well-known traditions is that of moai—groups of friends or acquaintances who regularly meet to share experiences, support each other, and strengthen their sense of unity. These groups are not just practical reference points but also a source of comfort and motivation. Knowing you can rely on someone in times of need, as well as share moments of joy, contributes to emotional well-being and the feeling of living a meaningful life. Moai are especially significant for the elderly in Okinawa, who attribute their happiness and long life not only to a healthy lifestyle but also to the network of friendships surrounding them. This type of social bond fosters a strong sense of security and usefulness, particularly when contributing to others' well-being.

Ikigai as a Contribution to Others

Ikigai is not limited to what brings personal joy but extends to how one's actions can enrich the lives of others. In Japan, individual well-being is often intertwined with collective well-being, and many find their purpose in contributing to activities that improve others' lives.

For example, a craftsman working passionately to create traditional items not only finds satisfaction in their work but also feels fulfilled knowing their craft helps preserve local culture. Similarly, a farmer providing quality food to their community derives energy and meaning from their contribution, aware that their work has a positive impact on many people. These small, everyday actions become a fundamental pillar of living according to one's Ikigai.

Relationships as the Foundation of Ikigai

Authentic and meaningful connections not only support our sense of purpose but enrich it. In Japan, values such as mutual respect, empathy, and loyalty are the foundation of interpersonal relationships, creating fertile ground for cultivating Ikigai.For instance, many elders find their reason for living by helping younger generations, sharing their experiences and wisdom. In return, younger people respond with care and gratitude, creating a generational balance that enriches both sides. This sense of exchange and connection also manifests in simple daily habits. For example, neighbors exchanging homemade gifts or helping each other during local events create an environment that reinforces unity and meaning, even through seemingly ordinary gestures.

The Power of Small Actions

In Japan, it's not necessary to perform grand gestures to feel part of something larger. Often, small daily actions build meaningful relationships and provide a sense of purpose. For example, an elder sharing their garden harvest with neighbors not only demonstrates generosity but also strengthens trust and collaboration. These small gestures fuel their Ikigai, giving them daily motivation to continue passionately dedicating themselves to their activities.

Lessons for the Modern World

In contemporary societies, often more individualistic, the Japanese approach to social bonds can offer valuable lessons. Even in urban contexts, people can find ways to build meaningful support networks. Joining local groups, such as sports clubs, cultural organizations, or neighborhood associations, is a way to feel connected to others and enrich your life. Another fundamental aspect is the value of mutual support. Even small actions, like taking time to listen to a friend or helping an acquaintance with a task, can strengthen social bonds and make life more meaningful. The essence of this philosophy is that personal well-being and collective well-being are deeply intertwined.

Conclusion

Ikigai is deeply tied to human relationships and the sense of connection with others. Through support networks, small acts of kindness, and the joy of sharing life's moments, people can build a more meaningful and fulfilling life. This perspective reminds us that our purpose does not exist in isolation—it is enriched by relationships and the contributions we make to others. Integrating this vision into daily life not only improves personal well-being but also enriches the social fabric around us, making life fuller for everyone.

Fears and Insecurities: How to Overcome Them

The path to discovering your Ikigai is not always straightforward. One of the most common obstacles is the fears and insecurities that may arise along the way. The fear of failure, not being enough, or choosing the wrong path is something many of us face. However, these emotions, if approached with the right mindset, can become valuable tools for personal growth and for discovering your purpose

The Roots of Fears and Insecurities

The fears and insecurities we encounter in our search for Ikigai often stem from external expectations or past experiences. For instance, the fear of failure may come from previous unsuccessful attempts, while insecurity about one's worth may be fueled by comparisons with others or unrealistic standards imposed by society.

These feelings are natural and human but can become barriers if we let them take over. For example, someone who dreams of starting a creative business might feel paralyzed by thoughts of not being talented enough or not having the necessary resources. These doubts, if left unaddressed, risk halting any progress toward achieving their Ikigai.

Recognizing and Accepting Your Fears

The first step to overcoming fears is to acknowledge and accept them. Denying or suppressing these feelings will only amplify their power. Instead, accepting that you feel fear allows you to face it with greater awareness and courage. A useful exercise is to write down all the fears you feel about your journey to Ikigai on a sheet of paper. You might discover that many of these fears are based on unrealistic perceptions or assumptions with no concrete foundation. For example, if you fear you're not skilled enough in a certain area, you could ask yourself: "What can I do to improve my skills?" This kind of reflection helps you transform a paralyzing fear into actionable steps.

The Role of Action in Overcoming Fears

Fears often lose their power when we start taking small steps toward what we desire. Action, even minimal, is a powerful tool for breaking the cycle of inaction. For example, if you're afraid of pursuing a new career, you could begin with activities that allow you to explore it gradually, such as attending workshops, reading books on the subject, or speaking with people who work in that field. The principle of Kaizen—continuous improvement through small steps—can be very useful in this context. Every small progress strengthens your confidence and brings you closer to your Ikigai, proving that fears can be faced and overcome.

Facing the Fear of Others' Judgments

One of the most common fears is the fear of others' judgment. Many avoid pursuing their Ikigai because they're afraid of being criticized or misunderstood by those around them. This is especially true when one's purpose deviates from the expectations of family, friends, or society.

To overcome this fear, it's important to remember that your Ikigai is unique and personal. No one else can define it for you. Focus on what makes you feel alive and in harmony with yourself, rather than seeking others' approval. Surround yourself with people who support you and share similar values, as having a network of trusted individuals can be crucial for maintaining motivation.

Managing Perfectionism and the Fear of Failure

Perfectionism is another form of fear that can hinder the discovery of your Ikigai. The idea of having to do everything perfectly may lead you to procrastinate or avoid new experiences altogether. However, failure is not the end of the journey—it's a natural part of the growth process.

Try to view mistakes as opportunities to learn. For instance, if you start a project and don't achieve the desired results right away, reflect on what you've learned and how you can improve. Every step, even if imperfect, brings you closer to your purpose. Remember that Ikigai is not a final destination but a journey that evolves with you.

Practical Tools to Face Your Fears

Overcoming fears and insecurities requires a mindful and practical approach. Here are some strategies to help you build resilience and make progress on your path to Ikigai.

Write a Fear Journal

Take time to write down all the fears that are holding you back. Don't just list them—analyze them: What is their origin? Are they based on past experiences or irrational worries? For example, if you're afraid of changing jobs, ask yourself:

- "What's the worst-case scenario?"
- "How could I handle it?"

Writing allows you to emotionally distance yourself from your fear, reducing its intensity and transforming it into a manageable problem.

Visualize Success

Imagine what your life will look like once you've overcome a specific fear. For instance, if you're afraid of public speaking, visualize yourself speaking confidently and receiving applause. Focus on positive details—the environment, feelings of satisfaction, and sense of accomplishment.

This exercise not only reduces anxiety but also motivates you to take action toward achieving that desired state.

Seek Inspiration

Read stories of people who have faced and overcome similar challenges. For example, you might learn about an entrepreneur who failed multiple times before finding success or an artist who overcame rejection to achieve their Ikigai. These stories show that fear is common and overcoming it is possible, providing a practical model to follow.

Practice Gratitude

Focus on what you've already achieved and your inner strengths. Write down three things you're grateful for every day, such as a personal quality, a goal you've accomplished, or the support of a loved one. This practice helps maintain a positive perspective, strengthening your self-confidence and determination to move forward.

Conclusion

Fears and insecurities are natural obstacles that may arise during the journey toward discovering your Ikigai, but they don't have to become insurmountable barriers. Recognizing, accepting, and addressing them with concrete actions allows you to transform them into opportunities for growth. Every step you take, no matter how small, is a step toward a more authentic and meaningful life. Your Ikigai is not an unreachable goal but a reality you can build day by day by overcoming your fears and embracing your potential..

The "I Don't Have Time" Syndrome

One of the most common obstacles to discovering your Ikigai is the perception of not having enough time. How often have you thought, "I'd love to dedicate myself to what I love, but I don't have time"? This syndrome, so widespread in modern life, can easily become an excuse that keeps us away from our purpose. However, it's often not a real lack of time but a matter of priorities, organization, and awareness. Overcoming this syndrome doesn't mean "finding" more time but learning to use it more intentionally.

The Myth of Not Having Enough Time

Many people feel overwhelmed by daily commitments, convinced they don't have room to make time for what they love. However, time is a universal resource: everyone has 24 hours in a day. The difference isn't in the amount of time available but in how we use it.

The feeling of "not having time" often comes from unconscious habits, such as spending hours on social media, procrastinating, or engaging in low-value tasks that don't contribute to our well-being or goals.

For instance, someone working 40 hours a week and caring for their family might still find free time—perhaps just half an hour a day—that is often spent on passive activities like watching TV or scrolling on their phone. Identifying and reclaiming these moments is the first step to overcoming the "I don't have time" syndrome.

Recognizing True Priorities

To start dedicating yourself to your Ikigai, you first need to identify what is truly important to you. This means distinguishing between what is urgent and what is meaningful. Urgent tasks often take up much of our time, leaving little room for activities that bring value and significance to our lives. For example, if your Ikigai involves writing, consider how much time you actually dedicate to this activity compared to daily tasks like answering emails or browsing online. A useful exercise is to list your weekly activities and ask yourself:

- "Does this activity contribute to my purpose?"
- "Does it bring me closer to my Ikigai?"

This process helps you redistribute your time more intentionally.

Small Changes, Big Results

Once you've identified your priorities, the next step is to create space for them. You don't need drastic changes or entire days devoted to your Ikigai—small daily moments are enough.

For example, you can start by dedicating just 10–15 minutes a day to something you love. If your purpose is painting, keep your supplies ready and use those few minutes to paint, even just a small detail.

The principle of Kaizen—continuous improvement through small steps—is particularly helpful. Each small progress motivates you to keep going and proves that even a few minutes a day can lead to significant changes over time.

Managing Distractions

Distractions are one of the main reasons people feel like they don't have enough time. Phone notifications, social media, emails, and other daily interruptions can easily consume hours of your day without you even realizing it. To overcome the "I don't have time" syndrome, it's essential to reduce these distractions. For instance, you can set specific times during the day to check emails or use social media, rather than doing so continuously. You can also use time management tools like timers or apps that block distractions to help you focus on what truly matters. Creating a distraction-free environment, such as a dedicated corner of your home for meaningful activities, can make a big difference.

Learning to Say No

Another reason for the "I don't have time" syndrome is the tendency to say "yes" to everything. Taking on too many commitments can leave you exhausted and without energy to dedicate to your Ikigai. Learning to say no, respectfully but firmly, is a crucial skill for protecting your time.

For example, if someone asks you to participate in a project or activity that isn't aligned with your goals, consider it carefully before agreeing.

Ask yourself: "Does this commitment contribute to my Ikigai, or does it take me further away from it?" Saying no isn't selfish; it's about prioritizing what's most important to you

Creating an Intentional Routine

An effective way to overcome the feeling of not having time is to create a routine that includes moments dedicated to your Ikigai. Plan your time as you would for an important appointment: mark on your calendar the moments when you'll focus on your passions or goals. For example, you could set aside 30 minutes each morning or evening to work on what you're passionate about, whether it's reading, meditating, writing, or exercising. Even simple rituals, like starting the day with a list of goals or a brief gratitude session, can help you stay focused and intentional..

Conclusion

The "I don't have time" syndrome is a common but surmountable obstacle. Time is a limited resource, but it can be managed more effectively through awareness, organization, and small changes.By recognizing your priorities, eliminating distractions, and creating space for what is meaningful, you can move closer to your Ikigai without overhauling your entire life. Start with just a few minutes a day, manage your time intentionally, and you'll find that even in the busiest life, there is room for what truly matters.

The Influence of Society and External Expectations

One of the most insidious obstacles in the search for your Ikigai is the influence of society and external expectations. We live in a world that often defines success by predetermined standards: a prestigious job, a high salary, a perfect family. While these criteria provide a point of reference, they can steer us away from our authentic purpose, pushing us to live according to others' desires rather than our own deepest values.

Society's Expectations and Their Impact

From a young age, many of us are exposed to a set of expectations that shape how we think and act. School teaches us to follow a linear path to "success": get good grades, find a stable job, build a family. While these are valid aspirations, they can become limiting if they don't reflect our true desires.

For instance, you might have grown up in a family that views a medical career as the only respectable path. Even if you have a natural talent for art or music, you may feel compelled to pursue science studies to meet your parents' expectations.

This kind of external pressure can lead you to ignore what truly makes you happy and live a life that doesn't feel like your own. The consequences of conforming to these expectations often include dissatisfaction, stress, and, in some cases, burnout. Living a life built on what others expect can make you feel disconnected from yourself, pulling you further from your Ikigai.

The Role of Social Comparison

Social comparisons further amplify society's influence. With the rise of social media, we're constantly exposed to images of people who seem to "have it all": successful careers, dream vacations, perfect relationships. This constant exposure can create feelings of inadequacy and push us to chase goals that don't align with our true desires. For example, you may feel pressured to start a business or pursue a trendy career simply because you see others doing it. However, what works for someone else might not align with your purpose. Continuously comparing yourself to others distracts you from focusing on what is genuinely meaningful to you.

How to Free Yourself from External Expectations

Overcoming society's influence and external expectations requires reflection and awareness. Here are some strategies to reconnect with your Ikigai:

1. **Identify What Truly Matters to You**

2. Take time to reflect on your values, interests, and personal aspirations. Ask yourself: "What truly makes me happy? What activities give me energy and satisfaction?" Write a list of what you love to do and what excites you. This exercise will help you distinguish your authentic desires from those imposed externally.

3. **Question Expectations**

Ask yourself where the expectations you feel come from. Are they truly yours, or were they inherited from family, friends, or society? For instance, if you feel pressured to pursue a traditional career, consider whether this choice reflects what you genuinely want or if you're trying to meet a social norm.

4. **Define Your Personal Success**

Success isn't universal: what it means to you might differ from what it means to others. Perhaps success for you is having more free time for your family or cultivating a hobby rather than earning a promotion. Defining your concept of success allows you to carve out a personal path that aligns with your Ikigai.

Facing Others' Judgments

One of the biggest challenges in breaking free from external expectations is dealing with others' judgments. You may fear that, by following your Ikigai, others will see you as unambitious, unrealistic, or even selfish.

However, it's important to remember that your purpose is unique and cannot be fully understood by those who don't share your values or experiences.

To overcome this fear, try communicating your choices clearly and assertively. Explain to those around you why you're following a particular path and how it makes you happy. People often respect decisions made with conviction and sincerity, even if they don't fully understand them.

Surround Yourself with the Right People

The support of a network of people who share your values and approach to life can make a big difference. Seek out individuals who encourage and support you in pursuing your Ikigai. This might mean joining groups or communities with similar interests, attending events or workshops, or simply building meaningful relationships with those who appreciate your authenticity.

Reconnecting with Your Ikigai

Rediscovering your Ikigai means gradually freeing yourself from the chains of external expectations. This doesn't mean completely ignoring society but finding a balance between what matters to you and what is required by the world around you.

Living according to your Ikigai takes courage, but the result is a more authentic and fulfilling life.

Conclusion

External expectations and societal influence can pose significant obstacles in the search for your Ikigai. However, with awareness, reflection, and the courage to be authentic, it is possible to break free from these pressures and build a life that reflects your values and deepest aspirations. By focusing on what brings you happiness and meaning, you can find a balance between the external world and your inner self, drawing closer to your true purpose.

Practical Application

The Practice of Ikigai

Exercises to Reflect on What You Love to Do

The discovery of your Ikigai begins with a simple yet fundamental question: "What do I love to do?" In the fast pace of daily life, it's easy to lose sight of the activities that bring us joy and ignite a spark within. This first step toward Ikigai requires a pause—a moment of reflection dedicated entirely to yourself. Below are practical exercises to help you identify what you truly love, guiding you toward greater awareness of your passions and inclinations.

1. The Passion List

Start by creating a list of things you love to do. Set aside time for this exercise in a quiet, distraction-free environment. Take a sheet of paper or a notebook and write a simple question in the center: "What do I truly love to do?"

Begin writing down any activities, big or small, that come to mind. These could range from simple things like reading a book, walking in nature, or cooking, to more complex pursuits such as playing an instrument, writing a novel, or working on group projects. Don't worry about being "logical" or "reasonable."

The goal of this exercise is to bring out what makes you feel alive, free from filters or judgment.

When you're done, review your list and note which activities evoke the strongest emotions. Highlight those that resonate with you most and try to describe why you enjoy them. For instance, if you wrote "writing," ask yourself: "What do I love about writing? Is it expressing my ideas? The creative process? Or the satisfaction of completing something?"

2. A Journey to the Past

Authentic passions often have their roots in childhood or adolescence—times when we were free from external expectations and followed our interests with spontaneity. Reflecting on what you loved as a child can reveal long-lost passions.

Ask yourself:

- What activities did I enjoy as a child? For example, building things, drawing, inventing stories, or exploring nature for hours.

- What were my dreams and aspirations? Perhaps you dreamed of being an explorer, artist, or teacher.
- What did I do without ever getting bored?

Write down your answers and observe whether there are connections to what you do today or activities you might want to revisit. This exercise can uncover forgotten or overlooked passions that may still be part of your Ikigai.

3. The Flow Technique

The concept of "flow," developed by psychologist Mihaly Csikszentmihalyi, refers to a state of complete immersion in an activity where you lose track of time and are fully concentrated on what you're doing. Reflecting on moments when you've experienced this sensation can help you identify what you love.

Ask yourself:

- When do I feel completely immersed in what I'm doing?
- What activities make me lose track of time?
- Which tasks give me energy instead of draining it?

Write a list of these activities and think about how they connect to your passions. For example, if you lose track of time while cooking, you might discover that creating something with your hands is an essential part of your Ikigai.

4. The Emotion Journal

A practical way to explore what you love is to keep an emotion journal for one or two weeks. Each day, write down the activities you performed and the emotions you felt while doing them. You can use a simple table with three columns:

1. Activity performed
2. How I felt during this activity
3. Did I enjoy it? Why?

This exercise will help you identify which activities give you positive energy and which leave you indifferent or drained. After a week, review your journal and look for patterns or trends.

You'll notice that certain activities repeatedly appear as sources of joy and satisfaction—these are key clues to your Ikigai.

5. Asking for Feedback

Sometimes, the people around us can see aspects of ourselves that we miss. Asking for feedback from those who know you well—friends, family, or colleagues—can provide a fresh perspective on what you're passionate about.

Ask questions like:

- What activities do you think make me happy?
- What do you think I'm particularly good at?
- When do you see me the most enthusiastic or inspired?

Listening to these responses with an open mind can help you discover new ideas or confirm existing intuitions. For example, a friend might say you seem happiest when talking about travel, or they may notice a particular energy when you organize events.

6. Experimenting and Exploring

Finally, one way to discover what you love is by trying new activities. If you're unsure of your passions, dedicate time to exploring something new—a course, hobby, or project. For instance, you could enroll in a painting class, attend a photography workshop, or join a book club. The key is to maintain an open mind and not fear failure. Every experience will give you insight into what you like (or don't like), bringing you closer to your Ikigai.

Conclusion

Reflecting on what you love to do is an essential step in discovering your Ikigai. The exercises provided here will help you explore your passions, rediscover forgotten desires, and gain a deeper understanding of what truly makes you happy. Take the time to complete these activities with intention and curiosity—your Ikigai isn't an immediate answer but a journey of personal discovery.

Identifying Your Talents and Skills

One of the key elements in discovering your Ikigai is recognizing your talents and abilities. Knowing what you're good at allows you to understand not only what you can offer the world but also how to best express your uniqueness. This process of self-exploration requires introspection, openness, and a bit of experimentation. It's not always immediate, but with the right tools, it's possible to identify your skills and leverage them to create a life filled with meaning.

The Connection Between Talent and Ikigai

In the context of Ikigai, talents represent what you naturally excel at or have refined through time and experience. Recognizing your abilities helps you identify the intersection between what you love to do and what you do well. For example, you might love painting, but if you also have a talent for combining colors and perspectives, this skill allows you to turn a passion into a meaningful contribution to the world. Talents aren't always obvious. Sometimes, what we're good at feels so natural that we take it for granted. For instance, you might be particularly skilled at solving complex problems but not consider this a talent because it feels "normal" to you. Recognizing this is the first step to integrating your abilities into your Ikigai.

Exercises to Discover Your Talents

Here are some practical activities to help you identify your talents and abilities:

1. **Reflect on Past Successes**

A good starting point is to analyze your past experiences. Take a sheet of paper and list moments when you felt accomplished or received praise for something you did.

Ask yourself:

- What projects or activities have I been successful in?

- What skills did I use in those moments?

- What positive feedback have I received from others? For example, if you successfully organized an event, you might discover you have a talent for planning and time management. If you've helped a friend solve a complex problem, it might reveal critical thinking or empathy skills.

2. **Ask for Feedback from Others.**

Often, those who know us well can see talents we don't recognize ourselves. Ask trusted friends, family, or colleagues about the abilities they see in you. You can ask questions like:

- What do you think I'm particularly good at?

- What qualities do you admire in me?

- In what situations would you turn to me for advice or help?

For instance, a colleague might highlight your ability to motivate others, while a friend might point out your knack for storytelling. This feedback offers valuable external perspectives to identify your strengths.

3. **Explore Your "Natural Flow"**

The activities you excel at often overlap with those where you easily enter a state of "flow"—a sense of total immersion and concentration. Reflecting on activities where time seems to fly can help you identify natural skills you use effortlessly.

Ask yourself:

- What activities come easily to me but seem difficult for others?

- When do I feel fully engaged and satisfied?

- Which tasks energize me rather than drain me?

For example, if you enjoy writing and easily organize your ideas, you might have a talent for communication. If working in a team excites you and you find creative solutions to problems, you might be a natural leader.

4. Experiment and Learn

If you're unsure of your talents, one of the most effective strategies is to experiment with new activities. Often, we discover hidden abilities only when we step outside our usual experiences. Trying new experiences not only helps you explore areas you hadn't considered but also allows you to develop skills that can become integral to your Ikigai. Here are some ideas to get started:

- **Take a Cooking Class**: If you love food and creativity, a cooking class might reveal a talent for preparing unique dishes. You might discover a passion for baking, traditional cuisine, or even the art of food presentation.

- **Try DIY or Crafts**: Test your hands-on skills with DIY projects, woodworking, or creating handmade items. For example, try building a simple piece of furniture, making jewelry, or crafting home decorations.

- **Join a Creative Writing Workshop**: If you enjoy storytelling or have always wanted to put your thoughts on paper, a creative writing workshop could uncover a passion for narrative, poetry, or copywriting.

- **Explore a Physical Activity or Sport**: Try something new like yoga, climbing, or dance. You might discover a talent for movement, coordination, or group energy.

- **Get Involved in Community Projects**: Participating in cultural or local initiatives can test your organizational, social, or leadership skills.

- **Dive into Technology or Digital Fields**: Explore programming, graphic design, or video editing courses. For instance, creating a blog or video about your project might reveal talents in digital storytelling.

- **Pursue Music or Art**: Take lessons in painting, sculpture, or music if you've always been drawn to the arts. You might find a talent for visual creations or playing an instrument that becomes a significant part of your expression.Each new experience, even if brief, broadens your horizons and uncovers facets of yourself you didn't know existed. The key is to step out of your comfort zone: every attempt, even without immediate success, is progress in understanding who you are and what you're capable of.

Connecting Talents to Your Ikigai

Once you've identified your talents, the next step is to reflect on how they can contribute to your Ikigai.

Ask yourself:

- How can I use these abilities in ways that bring me satisfaction?
- What problems or needs can I address using what I'm good at?
- Can I combine these skills with what I love to do?

For example, if you've discovered a talent for photography and love traveling, you might explore the potential to become a travel photographer. If you have natural empathy and enjoy helping others, you might consider working in personal support or counseling.

Overcoming Insecurities About Your Abilities

Even after identifying your talents, it's natural to feel uncertain or doubt their value. These feelings can arise from comparisons with others, fear of not being good enough, or the belief that your abilities aren't "special." However, it's important to remember that every talent, big or small, is meaningful and can be developed. What matters is not starting with perfect skills, but the dedication and effort to improve them. If you feel insecure about your abilities, begin by dedicating time and resources to cultivate them.

Examples

- **Writing**: If you love writing but don't feel confident, consider enrolling in a creative writing course or attending workshops to develop your style. You could also start a personal blog to practice and receive feedback from readers.
- **Public Speaking**: If you fear speaking in public but have a natural aptitude for explaining complex concepts, join a club like Toastmasters or attend storytelling events. Each opportunity to practice will boost your confidence.

- **Art or Crafts:** If you've discovered a love for art but feel unsure about your skills, take courses in painting, ceramics, or design. Practice and feedback from instructors often help strengthen your abilities.

- **Technology:** If you're curious about exploring the digital world, try courses in graphic design, programming, or video editing. Small projects, like creating a personal website or a short video, can build your confidence.

Each step toward improvement, no matter how small, reinforces your self-esteem and demonstrates your ability to grow and refine your talents. Insecurity often stems from unrealistic expectations; combat it by focusing on progress, not perfection. Remember, your journey is unique, and every effort you make brings you closer to your Ikigai.

Conclusion

Identifying your talents and abilities is a fundamental step on the path to discovering your Ikigai. Recognizing what you're good at not only helps you appreciate your uniqueness but also provides a compass to guide you toward a meaningful and fulfilling future. Through reflection, feedback from others, and the exploration of new experiences, you can uncover a world of potential within yourself, ready to be expressed and shared with the world.

Recognizing the Needs of the World Around You

One of the fundamental aspects of Ikigai is the connection between what you love, your talents, and the needs of the world around you. This pillar, often referred to as "mission," invites you to reflect on how you can use your skills and passions to serve others and address real needs. Understanding the needs of the world not only helps you find deeper meaning in your work and actions but also allows you to create more authentic connections with people and the environment around you.

Why Recognizing the World's Needs Is Important

One of the fundamental aspects of Ikigai is the connection between what you love, your talents, and the needs of the world around you. This pillar, often referred to as "mission," invites you to reflect on how you can use your skills and passions to serve others and address real needs. Understanding the needs of the world not only helps you find deeper meaning in your work and actions but also allows you to create more authentic connections with people and the environment around you.

Why Recognizing the World's Needs Is Important

We live in an interconnected society where every choice we make impacts others. Recognizing the world's needs helps you move beyond your individual perspective to embrace a broader vision focused on collective well-being. This approach not only enriches your Ikigai but also creates opportunities to make a meaningful difference. For example, if you're a teacher passionate about education, you might discover children in your community who struggle to access learning resources. Recognizing this need could inspire you to offer free tutoring or create an educational program accessible to everyone. Such a contribution not only fulfills a real need but also gives you a profound sense of accomplishment.

How to Identify the World's Needs

Recognizing the needs of the world requires observation, empathy, and a practical approach. Here are some strategies to get started:

1. **Observe Your Environment**

Pay attention to what's happening around you. What are the most evident problems in your community, workplace, or society in general? You might notice a lack of resources for vulnerable groups, the need for environmental initiatives, or a greater demand for support in areas like mental health or education. For example, you might realize your neighborhood lacks a safe space for young people. If you're passionate about mentoring and organization, you could start a project to create a recreational center or support program.

2. Ask Directly

The world's needs aren't always immediately visible. Sometimes, the best solution is to ask people directly what's needed. Speak with friends, colleagues, or community members to better understand their challenges and needs.

Questions to ask:

- What are the main problems you face in your daily life?
- What do you think is missing in our community or your work sector?
- How can I contribute meaningfully?

These conversations can provide valuable insights and reveal opportunities you hadn't considered before.

3. Seek Inspiration from Success Stories

Reading stories of people who have made a difference in the world can help you identify areas where you could contribute. For instance, you might learn about an entrepreneur who started a business to reduce food waste or an artist who used their creativity to raise awareness about social issues.

Ask yourself: "How can I adapt my talents and passions to address a similar need in my reality?"

4. Examine Global Issues

In addition to looking locally, consider the global issues that matter to you. Topics such as climate change, poverty, access to education, and gender inequality are just a few of the challenges requiring innovative solutions and motivated individuals. Reflect on how your skills could address one of these issues on a larger scale.

For example:

- If you have technological expertise, you could develop an app that raises awareness about eco-friendly practices.

- If you're a communication expert, you could launch a campaign to raise awareness about an issue you care about.

Connecting Your Talents to the Needs of the World

Once you've identified the needs of the world, the next step is understanding how your talents and passions can help address them. This process requires creativity and reflection. Ask yourself:

- What problems do I care about the most?

- How can I use my skills to make a difference?

- What small step can I take today to start contributing?

For instance, if you have a talent for cooking and know that many people in your community lack access to nutritious meals, you could start an initiative to prepare and distribute food to those in need. Alternatively, if you're an engineer passionate about the environment, you might design sustainable technological solutions for your city.

Overcoming Challenges in Addressing the World's Needs

Responding to the world's needs can feel overwhelming, but you don't have to tackle everything alone or solve global problems in one grand gesture. Even a small, targeted contribution can have a significant impact, whether locally or globally. Start by focusing on what's within your reach and begin small, building progressively.

Examples

- If you're passionate about environmental sustainability, you don't need to establish a major organization right away. Start by reducing waste in your daily life, involving friends and neighbors in initiatives like composting, or organizing neighborhood clean-up days.

- If education is your passion, instead of aiming for large-scale reforms, begin by mentoring a student or helping someone with their studies.

Collaboration is another essential element. You don't have to do everything on your own. Join groups that share your values or work with people whose skills complement yours. For example, if you want to address food insecurity in your community, collaborate with local organizations or create a network of donors to distribute meals.

Don't let the enormity of the problems discourage you. Instead of focusing on the complexity of the bigger picture, concentrate on what you can do in your immediate context. Every small step counts. Even simple actions, like gathering opinions to better understand your community's needs, can become a significant starting point for creating lasting impact.

Remember: Change is built step by step, with patience and intentionality.

Conclusion

Recognizing the needs of the world around you is a crucial element in discovering your Ikigai. This process enables you to connect your passions and abilities to a larger mission, giving meaning to your life while contributing to collective well-being. Start with small steps: observe your environment, talk to people, seek inspiration, and reflect on how your talents can make a difference. You'll find that your Ikigai is not just a personal journey but also a valuable contribution to the world around you.Finding the Balance Between Passion, Vocation, Mission, and Profession.

Ikigai lies at the intersection of four key elements:

1. What you love to do (passion).
2. What you are good at (vocation).
3. What the world needs (mission).
4. What you can be paid for (profession).

Finding the balance between these pillars is not always immediate, but it represents the heart of your Ikigai—your reason for being. This process requires introspection, practice, and a deep understanding of yourself and the context around you.

Understanding the Intersection of the Four Pillars

Each of the four Ikigai pillars plays a unique role in giving your life meaning:

- **Passion**: What excites you and makes you feel alive. This is the emotional drive that motivates you to joyfully engage in activities.

- **Vocation**: What you naturally excel at or have developed through experience. This represents your unique contribution to the world.

- **Mission**: The world's needs that resonate with your personal values, giving you a sense of a larger purpose.

- **Profession**: What you can be paid for, the practical side that allows you to sustain yourself financially.

Your Ikigai is found at the center of these elements, where each integrates with the others, creating a balance between personal fulfillment, social impact, and economic sustainability.

The Risk of Imbalance

When one pillar is missing or dominates the others, your Ikigai can feel out of balance. For example:

- If you focus only on passion and mission, you may feel inspired but financially unsustainable.

- If you focus only on vocation and profession, you may achieve financial success but feel a lack of purpose or enthusiasm.

- If you pursue a mission without considering vocation, you may have good intentions but feel unskilled or unfulfilled.

The goal is to find a balance that satisfies both your heart and mind, blending purpose with practical needs.

Exercises to Find Your Balance

To discover your point of balance, it's helpful to reflect on each pillar and work to connect them. Here are some practical exercises to guide you:

1. Draw the Ikigai Diagram

Draw four overlapping circles on a sheet of paper, one for each pillar: passion, vocation, mission, and profession. Write inside each circle what you believe represents each element in your life.

For example:

- In **passion**, list activities you love and that excite you.

- In **vocation**, list what you're good at.

- In **mission**, describe the needs of the world that inspire you.

- In **profession**, list how you could make a living using your skills.

Observe where the circles overlap and identify connections. For example, if you love teaching, excel at communication, and believe in the importance of education, you could explore careers or projects related to training and development.

2. Analyze Your Daily Activities

Spend a week tracking how you spend your time. Divide your daily activities into four categories:

- Activities that you are passionate about.
- Activities in which you feel you excel.
- Activities that meet a need.
- Activities for which you are paid.

Ask yourself: "Which activities fall into multiple categories?" These areas might bring you closer to your Ikigai. For instance, if helping colleagues at work brings you joy, utilizes your skills, and meets a need, it could be worth exploring further.

3. Prototype Your Ikigai

If you've identified a potential point of balance, experiment with it on a small scale before fully committing.

Examples:

- If you think your Ikigai is related to design, start by working on small projects for friends or family.
- If you're interested in writing, create a blog or write freelance articles.

These experiments allow you to test the sustainability of your ideas and evaluate how you feel when combining passion, vocation, mission, and profession.

Accepting That Balance Can Change

Your Ikigai isn't static—it changes with you and the circumstances of your life. What works today may not work ten years from now, and that's okay.

For instance, you might begin your career focusing on profession and gradually develop your mission as you gain experience. Or, you may discover new passions or world needs that transform your Ikigai over time.

The important thing is to continue reflecting and reevaluating your balance as you grow and as the world around you evolves.

Examples of Balanced Ikigai

To better understand how to integrate the four pillars (passion, vocation, mission, and profession), here are three practical examples illustrating different ways to find equilibrium.

1. The Technology Tutor

- **Passion**: Teaching others and simplifying technology.
- **Vocation**: Skill in breaking down complex technological concepts into simpler terms.
- **Mission**: Addressing the growing need for digital literacy, particularly among those less familiar with technology.
- **Profession**: Offering personalized or group courses to teach the practical use of digital tools like smartphones, computers, or software.

Example:

A technology tutor might organize weekly sessions for seniors, teaching them how to use messaging apps, social media platforms, or tools for safe online shopping. These lessons can significantly enhance their quality of life by helping them connect with loved ones and navigate the digital world more confidently.

2. The Sustainable Garden Designer

- **Passion**: Creating green spaces that promote well-being.
- **Vocation**: Talent for designing harmonious and functional environments.
- **Mission**: Meeting the need for more sustainable and eco-friendly green spaces, both in cities and private residences.
- **Profession**: Working as a sustainable garden designer, creating spaces that blend aesthetics with environmental consciousness.

Example:

The designer might specialize in creating vertical gardens or eco-friendly terraces using recycled materials and drought-resistant plants. These solutions are ideal for urban environments or areas facing challenging climate conditions, offering beauty and sustainability.

3. The Inclusive Sports Educator

- **Passion:** Promoting sports as a tool for inclusion and well-being.

- **Vocation:** Ability to motivate and work with individuals of all ages and physical abilities.

- **Mission:** Addressing the need for accessible sports programs for people with disabilities or mobility challenges.

- **Profession:** Working as a sports instructor, developing personalized programs or hosting inclusive sports events.

Example:

An inclusive sports educator might organize adaptive yoga classes, swimming lessons for individuals with reduced mobility, or fitness programs tailored to children with special needs. These activities foster a welcoming and stimulating environment for everyone, encouraging physical and emotional well-being.

Conclusion

Finding the balance between passion, vocation, mission, and profession is a journey that requires time and reflection, but the rewards of living according to your Ikigai are immeasurable. Each step you take toward this balance brings you closer to a life that is more meaningful, fulfilling, and aligned with your true self. The key is to be patient, open to change, and ready to explore. Your Ikigai is not just a destination—it is your path to a life of purpose. These examples demonstrate how Ikigai can be built around various combinations of interests, skills, and needs, offering unique pathways to a balanced and meaningful life. Each activity integrates passion, talent, a larger purpose, and a source of livelihood, showing that there are many ways to achieve balance.

Ikigai Journal: How to Track Your Progress

Discovering your Ikigai is a deeply personal journey filled with reflection, trial, and error. Like any path of growth, it requires time, commitment, and introspection. To stay focused and measure progress, one invaluable tool is the Ikigai journal. This journal is not just a place to record thoughts and ideas but also a practical way to monitor your path toward a more meaningful and balanced life.

Why an Ikigai Journal is Important

Writing regularly in a journal helps develop self-awareness and clarity. Daily or weekly reflections allow you to identify what works in your life, what needs improvement, and the concrete steps you're taking toward your Ikigai. Additionally, the journal serves as a visual reminder of your progress, motivating you to keep going even when challenges arise.

Through your journal, you can:

- Recognize and celebrate small victories.
- Identify areas where you feel stuck.
- Reevaluate priorities as you grow and your Ikigai evolves.
- Connect the four pillars—passion, vocation, mission, and profession—to your daily life.

How to Structure Your Ikigai Journal

An effective journal doesn't need to be complex. It can be a notebook, a digital document, or even an app. What matters is that it's organized to facilitate reflection and tracking. Here's a basic structure you can follow:

1. Daily Section: Daily Reflections

Spend a few minutes each day answering these questions:

- What was the most meaningful moment of my day?
- What activity brought me the most satisfaction or energy?
- What challenge did I encounter, and how did I handle it?

These reflections help you identify recurring patterns and understand which activities align with your Ikigai. For example, you might notice that you feel deeply fulfilled every time you assist a colleague at work, suggesting that your mission could be connected to supporting others.

2. Weekly Section: Summary and Planning

At the end of each week, take a moment to review what you wrote over the previous days. Answer these questions:

- Which activities brought me closer to my Ikigai this week?
- Which activities pulled me away from it?
- What steps can I take next week to better align with my purpose?

Use this section to set practical goals, such as dedicating more time to a passion or exploring new growth opportunities.

3. Monthly Section: Long-Term Review and Vision

Once a month, take a broader view of your progress by asking:

- Have I made progress toward my Ikigai?
- Which areas of my life need more attention?
- Is there anything I'd like to change or add to my journey?

This process helps you maintain perspective and make intentional adjustments to your path..

Practical Exercises for the Ikigai Journal

In addition to regular reflections, you can use your journal for specific exercises to explore and refine your Ikigai. Here are a few ideas:

The Passion List

Write a list of all the activities you love to do. Then, reflect on how these passions connect to the other Ikigai pillars. For example, if you love cooking, ask yourself:

- "Am I good at cooking?"
- "Is there a need in the world related to my passion for food?"
- "Can I turn this into a profession?"

2. The Ikigai Diagram

Draw the classic Ikigai diagram with four overlapping circles and use the journal to fill it with ideas and reflections. Each time you discover something new about yourself, update the diagram to better visualize how your pillars intersect.

3. The Progress Map

Dedicate a page in your journal to a "progress map," where you note every concrete step you take toward your Ikigai.

For example:

- "Spent 30 minutes today writing a short story."
- "Talked to a colleague about my interest in leadership."
- "Started exploring volunteer opportunities in my neighborhood."

Each step, no matter how small, is a milestone worth celebrating.

Using the Journal to Overcome Challenges

The path to Ikigai won't always be linear. There will be days when you feel confused or unmotivated. During these moments, the journal becomes even more vital, providing a safe space to process your feelings and regain clarity.

For example, if you feel stuck, try writing:

- "What is the biggest challenge I'm facing right now?
- "What options do I have to overcome it?"

This type of self-dialogue helps reframe difficulties as opportunities for growth.

Long-Term Benefits of the Journal

Over time, your Ikigai journal will become a valuable resource—an archive of your discoveries and successes. Rereading what you've written in previous months allows you to see how far you've come and how much closer you are to your purpose. It reminds you that, even during difficult moments, you've made progress and continued moving toward a more meaningful life.

Conclusion

The Ikigai journal is much more than a simple organizational tool—it's a personal guide that accompanies you on your journey toward authenticity and meaning. Writing regularly will help you explore, track, and celebrate every step toward your Ikigai. Over time, you'll see how your reflections and daily actions intertwine, bringing you closer to a life in harmony with yourself and the world around you.

Daily Practices of Mindfulness and Gratitude

Integrating mindfulness and gratitude into your daily routine is one of the most effective ways to align with your Ikigai. These practices not only help you live more consciously and in the present moment but also allow you to recognize the value of what you already have, fostering a sense of fulfillment and connection with yourself and the world. Mindfulness and gratitude are simple yet powerful tools that can transform your days, making your journey toward Ikigai smoother and more meaningful.

Why Mindfulness and Gratitude are Essential for Ikigai

Both mindfulness and gratitude are fundamental practices for those seeking to discover and live their Ikigai. Together, they provide tools to cultivate greater awareness and appreciation, forming a solid foundation for building a meaningful and fulfilling life.

Mindfulness and the Present Moment

Mindfulness teaches you to fully live in the present, freeing yourself from the weight of the past and constant worries about the future. Our days are often filled with distractions: work, phone notifications, and daily obligations. This state of distraction distances us from an awareness of what we're doing and, consequently, from what truly matters. Practicing mindfulness means slowing down and paying attention to each moment with intention. For example, during a simple walk, you can focus on the sensations in your body, the sounds around you, or the rhythm of your breath. This exercise allows you to experience life more deeply and helps you identify the activities and moments that bring you joy and satisfaction. Additionally, mindfulness is a powerful tool for recognizing your passions, talents, and purpose. When you are aware of your mental and emotional state, it becomes easier to understand what motivates you, energizes you, and what detracts from your Ikigai.

For instance, you might realize that you feel deeply fulfilled when helping others or that a creative activity like drawing allows you to become completely immersed in the present.

Gratitude and Appreciation

Gratitude invites you to shift your focus from what's missing in your life to what you already have. Often, we are so focused on future goals that we forget to appreciate the resources, experiences, and relationships around us.

For example, you might be grateful for a conversation with a friend, a warm meal, or the support of a colleague. Cultivating gratitude doesn't mean ignoring challenges or desires for improvement but recognizing the value of what you have in the present moment. This practice helps maintain a positive perspective, reduces stress, and fosters resilience. When you're grateful, you're more likely to notice opportunities and learn from experiences—even difficult ones.

Incorporating Mindfulness and Gratitude into Ikigai

Mindfulness and gratitude are not ends in themselves but tools that support you in your journey toward Ikigai. Mindfulness helps you clearly identify your passions and talents, while gratitude allows you to build on what you already have, strengthening your emotional and mental foundation. Together, they create a mindset that enables you to approach the path to a meaningful life with serenity..

Daily Mindfulness Practices

Here are some mindfulness techniques you can incorporate into your day:

1. **Mindful Breathing**

Mindful breathing is one of the simplest and most immediate practices for cultivating mindfulness. Spend a few minutes each day focusing on your breath, inhaling and exhaling slowly. You can do this anytime: in the morning upon waking, during a work break, or before bed.

For example, try this exercise:

- Sit in a comfortable position.

- Close your eyes and focus on the natural rhythm of your breath.

- Count to four as you inhale, hold your breath for two seconds, and then exhale, counting to six.

- Repeat for five minutes, letting go of thoughts and worries.

This practice calms the mind, reduces stress, and helps you reconnect with the present moment.

2. Mindfulness in Daily Activities

Bringing mindfulness to everyday activities is another way to live more consciously. For example, you can practice mindfulness while preparing coffee, washing dishes, or walking. Focus entirely on the activity you're performing: the aroma of the coffee, the sensation of water on your hands, or the rhythm of your steps.

This approach helps transform mundane actions into moments of presence, making them more meaningful and enjoyable.

3. Guided Meditation

If you're new to mindfulness, guided meditations can be a great starting point. Use apps like Headspace or Calm, or find free meditations online. Even just 10 minutes a day can make a difference, helping you cultivate greater calm and mental clarity.

Daily Gratitude Practices

Gratitude is a simple practice but requires intentionality. Here are some ideas to cultivate it in your routine:

1. Gratitude Journal

Make it a habit to write down three things you're grateful for each day. These can be major events, like a work success, or small things, like a friend's smile or a beautiful sunset. This exercise helps shift your focus from negative aspects of your day to positive ones, fostering a sense of contentment.

For example:

- "I'm grateful for my colleague's support during the meeting."• "I'm grateful for the time spent with my family at dinner."• "I'm grateful for the fresh air during my morning walk."

2. Expressing Gratitude

Another way to practice gratitude is to express it directly to others. Take time to thank someone for something they've done for you, whether it's a kind gesture or support during a challenging moment. You can do this in person, with a message, or by writing a letter. This act not only strengthens your bonds with others but also helps you recognize and appreciate the importance of relationships in your life.

3. Evening Reflection

At the end of the day, spend a few minutes reflecting on what went well. You can do this mentally or jot it down in your journal. Ask yourself:

- What was the best thing about my day?
- Who or what contributed to making it special?
- How can I bring more of these experiences into my life?

This practice helps you end the day on a positive note and start the next with a calmer and more optimistic mindset.

Conclusion

Daily mindfulness and gratitude practices are powerful tools for aligning with your Ikigai. Mindfulness helps you live with greater awareness and presence, while gratitude fosters a sense of fulfillment and resilience. Together, they create a strong foundation for identifying your passions, talents, and purpose. By integrating these practices into your daily routine, you'll not only enhance your journey toward Ikigai but also enrich your overall experience of life.

Combining Mindfulness and Gratitude

Mindfulness and gratitude are complementary practices that can be seamlessly integrated into a single routine. For example, you can begin your day with a meditation session where you focus on the things you're grateful for. Alternatively, during a mindful breathing exercise, you can reflect on a person or event that brought you joy.

Example Practice:

- **Inhale**: Think of one thing you're grateful for.
- **Exhale**: Imagine sending gratitude to that person or situation.

This approach blends the calming effect of mindfulness with the uplifting power of gratitude, creating a more profound experience.

Long-Term Benefits

Practicing mindfulness and gratitude daily helps manage stress and anxiety, while fostering a more positive and resilient attitude toward life. These practices strengthen your connection with yourself and the world around you, bringing you closer to your Ikigai. Over time, as these habits become integral to your routine, you'll find your journey toward balance and fulfillment more fluid and rewarding.

Creating Routines that Support Your Life's Purpose

Achieving your Ikigai isn't an overnight success; it's a journey requiring consistency, intention, and discipline. One of the most effective strategies for aligning with your purpose is establishing daily routines that support it. Routines provide a solid structure, reduce decision fatigue, and help you dedicate energy to what truly matters. Building positive habits aligned with your values is crucial for living in harmony with your Ikigai.

Why Routines Are Important for Ikigai

Routines provide stability and clarity, both essential for cultivating your purpose. Without a clear structure, it's easy to feel overwhelmed by daily distractions and lose sight of what truly matters. Routines keep you focused on activities that bring you closer to your Ikigai, helping you balance passion, vocation, mission, and profession.

For instance:

- If your Ikigai involves creative writing, a morning routine of writing for an hour ensures consistent progress.

- If your purpose involves mental and physical wellness, incorporating daily exercise and meditation can enhance your focus and resilience.

How to Build Routines That Reflect Your Ikigai

Here are practical steps to establish routines that align with your purpose:

1. **Identify Your Priorities**

Begin by clarifying what's most important to you. Ask yourself:

What activities bring me the most meaning?

How can I dedicate more time to what I love doing?

Which habits bring me closer to my Ikigai?

Write down a list of these activities and assess how much time you currently allocate to them. This reflection will help you pinpoint areas for improvement.

2. **Simplify and Optimize**

Freeing up time for what matters often involves eliminating unnecessary tasks. Streamline your day by:

Avoiding constant phone and social media checks.

Planning meals or daily activities in advance to reduce decision fatigue.

Blocking time for critical tasks and avoiding multitasking.

By reducing distractions, you'll create space for activities aligned with your Ikigai.

Practical Routines to Support Your Ikigai

Depending on your purpose and aspirations, here are routine ideas to help you along your path:

1. Morning Routine: **Starting the Day with Intention**

The morning is often the most productive part of the day. A sample routine might include:

- **Mindfulness:** Spend 5–10 minutes meditating or practicing deep breathing.

- **Visualizing Your Ikigai**: Reflect briefly on how the day's activities align with your purpose.
- **Creative or Productive Time**: Dedicate at least 30 minutes to an important project linked to your Ikigai, such as writing, designing, or planning.

2. Evening Routine: Reflecting and Recharging

The evening is a perfect time to wind down and prepare for the next day. A sample evening routine might include:

- **Reflection:** Write in your Ikigai journal about what you learned and achieved that day.
- **Gratitude Practice:** List three things you're grateful for.
- **Preparation:** Plan key tasks for the following day to start with clarity.

3. Weekly Routine: Reviewing and Planning

In addition to daily habits, reserve time each week to review your progress:

- Revisit your Ikigai journal to reflect on steps taken toward your purpose.
- Plan the upcoming week, ensuring time is set aside for meaningful activities.
- Assess successes and challenges from the past week to stay focused and motivated.

Overcoming Challenges in Establishing Routines

Building and maintaining new routines can be challenging, particularly in the beginning. Established habits take time to form, and the initial excitement often clashes with practical or mental obstacles. However, it's important to remember that change is a gradual process, and encountering difficulties along the way is completely normal. With the right strategies, even challenges can become opportunities for growth.

1. Start Small

One common mistake people make is trying to change too much, too quickly. This approach often leads to frustration and abandonment. Instead, focus on one or two new habits at a time.

- **Example**: If you want to incorporate physical exercise into your routine, start with a 10-minute daily walk rather than enrolling in an intensive gym program. Once this small habit takes root, you can build on it.

- Similarly, if you want to dedicate time to writing or meditation, begin with short 5–10 minute sessions.

This approach helps prevent overwhelm and builds the confidence needed to gradually expand your routines.

2. Be Flexible

Not all routines work for everyone, and what seems perfect on paper might not fit your real-life circumstances. Adopting a flexible and open approach is essential. If a routine doesn't work, don't see it as a failure; instead, view it as an opportunity to try a new approach.

- **Example**: If you find that reading in the evening leaves you too tired to focus, try shifting it to the morning or another time of day when you have more energy.

The goal isn't to rigidly stick to a predetermined plan but to create a structure that aligns with your needs and circumstances.

3. Celebrate Progress

Acknowledging and celebrating small milestones is essential for maintaining motivation. Each time you successfully carry out a new habit, even for a few consecutive days, take a moment to appreciate your effort.

- **Track Your Progress**: Use a journal or chart to log each time you complete an activity related to your routine.

- **Example**: If your goal is to write daily, celebrate each day you dedicate time to it, whether it's a few sentences or entire pages.

Consistency matters more than quantity, and recognizing your progress reinforces positive behavior and encourages you to continue.

Conclusion

Overcoming challenges in creating routines requires patience, adaptability, and a positive mindset. Start with simple, realistic steps, adjust your approach as needed, and celebrate each accomplishment, no matter how small.

Remember, success isn't measured by perfection but by consistency in pursuing what matters most to you. Over time, these routines will become an integral part of your life, bringing you closer to your Ikigai and helping you build a meaningful, fulfilling daily existence.

Practical Example: A Day Aligned with Ikigai

Imagine a person whose Ikigai revolves around promoting physical and mental well-being. Their day might look like this:

Morning:

- Begin the day with a brief meditation session to center the mind and set a positive tone.

- Engage in a yoga practice to boost energy and focus.

- Spend time preparing a structured plan for a fitness class or a wellness session.

Afternoon:

- Teach a yoga class or lead a workshop on stress management techniques.

- Dedicate time to meaningful interactions with participants, offering personalized guidance and encouragement.

Evening:

- Reflect on the day's interactions and experiences by journaling or meditating.

- Write down how their work contributed to others' well-being and note any moments of gratitude or growth.

This type of routine not only reinforces their Ikigai, but also provides the energy and motivation to keep pursuing it. By aligning their daily actions with their passion, vocation, mission, and profession, they create a life full of purpose and fulfillment

Conclusione

Creating routines that support your Ikigai is a vital step toward living an intentional and meaningful life. These routines help you maintain focus on your purpose while providing the structure needed to navigate challenges. With patience, self-reflection, and adaptability, you can build habits that bring you closer to your Ikigai each day, turning aspirations into tangible, fulfilling realities..

Finding Meaning and Satisfaction in Your Current Job

Many believe that finding meaning and satisfaction in their work requires a radical career change or embarking on a completely new path. However, fulfillment often comes not from the job itself but from how you engage with it. By making small mindset shifts, targeted reflections, and concrete actions, you can align your current role with your values, passions, and talents. In other words, you can uncover your Ikigai within the work you already do.

1. Understand the Meaning of Your Work

The first step in finding satisfaction is to understand how your role contributes to a larger picture. Even if your job seems routine or insignificant, reflecting on its impact can offer new perspectives. Ask yourself:

- What contribution does my work make to others?
- How does my role support the company or community?
- Which aspects of my work positively impact those around me?

For example, as an administrative assistant, your work might feel mundane at times. However, by organizing and facilitating processes, you empower your team to succeed in complex projects. Recognizing this contribution can give you a renewed appreciation for your role.

2. Identify the Positive Aspects of Your Job

Every job has aspects that can be sources of satisfaction, even amidst challenges. Take time to identify what you appreciate about your current role. You might discover:

- You enjoy collaborating with colleagues.
- You feel accomplished when solving complex problems.
- You take pride in the product or service you help deliver.

Writing these positives down can help shift your focus from frustrations to what energizes and motivates you.

3. Align Your Work with Your Values

Reflect on how your work can align with your personal values. Often, dissatisfaction stems from a misalignment between what you do and what matters to you.

For instance:

- If sustainability is important to you, you could propose eco-friendly initiatives like recycling programs in your office.

- If education is a core value, you could train new colleagues or contribute to creating learning materials for your team.

Small adjustments like these can make a big difference in making your work reflect who you are.

4. Personalize Your Role Through Job Crafting

Job crafting is the process of tailoring your role to make it more meaningful. You can adapt your responsibilities and approach to better suit your interests and abilities. This can be done in three main ways:

- **Modify Tasks**: Spend more time on activities you enjoy and try to delegate or reduce those you find less fulfilling.

- **Build Meaningful Relationships**: Strengthen connections with colleagues to create a more positive and collaborative environment.

- **Shift Your Perspective**: Focus on the positive impact your work creates.

For example, an accountant might find greater meaning by helping clients achieve financial security rather than just focusing on the numbers.

5. Develop Skills That Excite You

Invest in learning skills that resonate with your interests to make your job more engaging. Ask yourself:

- What skills would I like to deepen?

- How can I incorporate these skills into my current role?

For example, if you're passionate about communication, you could take a public speaking course and apply your new skills to presenting ideas or projects to your team. Personal growth not only enriches your work but also opens doors to new opportunities.

6. Find Purpose in Workplace Relationships

Building authentic relationships with colleagues can significantly enhance your work experience. Take time to:

- Actively listen to your coworkers and offer support when needed.
- Share successes and challenges to foster collaboration.
- Mentor less experienced colleagues, sharing your expertise to help them grow.

These relationships improve the work environment and help you see the value of your contributions.

7. Acknowledge Your Progress

Recognizing and celebrating your achievements is crucial for finding satisfaction in your current job. Every milestone, big or small, is a step forward. You can track your successes in a journal or dedicate a few minutes at the end of each day to reflect on your accomplishments.

For example, you might recognize the success of a well-conducted meeting, a completed project, or a satisfied client. This approach helps you focus on what's working and fosters a positive mindset toward your work.

Conclusion

Finding meaning and satisfaction in your current job is achievable, even without changing careers. Through reflection, small adjustments, and intentional actions, you can transform your role into something that aligns with your values and nurtures your Ikigai. By maintaining an open mindset and exploring new perspectives, you'll discover that meaning often lies hidden within the activities you already perform.

Strategies for Changing Careers and Following Your Ikigai

Changing careers is one of the most significant and challenging decisions you can face, but it can also be one of the most meaningful steps toward discovering your Ikigai. If your current job no longer aligns with your passions, talents, or values, embarking on a new career path offers an opportunity to align your professional life with your purpose. However, a career change requires careful planning, courage, and a clear vision of your aspirations. This guide provides practical strategies to help make this transition manageable and meaningful.

1. Reflect Deeply on the Reason for Change

Before taking any action, it's essential to understand why you feel the need to change careers. Asking the right questions can help you identify the causes of your dissatisfaction and clarify your true desires:

- What is missing in my current job?
- Which aspects of my work energize and satisfy me?
- What would my ideal workday look like?

Writing down your answers will give you a clearer view of which areas of your professional life need transformation. Additionally, this reflection will help you avoid making impulsive or poorly considered decisions.

2. Identify Your Destination: Your Ikigai

Changing careers isn't just about leaving something behind; it's about moving toward something new and meaningful. Therefore, having a clear vision of what you want to achieve is critical. Use the Ikigai framework to explore the four pillars:

- **What you love doing:** What activities excite you and make you lose track of time?
- **What you're good at:** What are your natural skills and abilities?
- **What the world needs:** What problems or needs inspire you?
- **What you can be paid for:** What job opportunities exist in your field of interest?

Find the intersections of these pillars to identify a new professional direction that aligns with your Ikigai.

3. Explore and Experiment

Once you've defined your goal, explore possibilities before committing to a drastic change. Here are some strategies to experiment with your Ikigai:

- **Side Projects:** Work on small projects that reflect your interests. For example, if you aspire to be a photographer, start taking photos in your free time and share them online.

- **Courses and Training:** Enroll in courses or workshops to gain skills in the field you're considering. This will help you determine if the new career aligns with your desires.

- **Volunteering or Internships:** Offer your time to collaborate with organizations or companies in your desired field. This experience will give you practical insight and help you build valuable connections.

4. Create a Transition Plan

Changing careers doesn't mean abandoning everything at once. A gradual approach can help you reduce risks and prepare better for the new path. Here's how to create a transition plan:

- **Set short- and long-term goals:** Define small, realistic steps to move toward your new career, such as completing specific training or gaining practical experience.

- **Save and plan financially:** Career changes can involve periods of financial instability. Create a savings plan or find ways to supplement your income during the transition.

- **Establish a timeline**: Set a timeframe for each phase of your plan to track progress and stay motivated.

5. Build a Support Network

Connections play a crucial role in your career transition. Build a network of people who can offer support, advice, or opportunities in the field you're considering:

- **Mentors**: Find individuals with experience in the career you want and ask for guidance on how to start.

- **Colleagues and Friends:** Share your goals with trusted individuals; they might offer useful ideas or connections.

- **Professional Communities**: Attend events, join online groups, or participate in conferences to build relationships in your new field.

6. Overcome the Fear of Change

It's normal to feel uncertain or afraid when facing a major transition like a career change. To overcome these fears:

- **Acknowledge your progress**: Celebrate every small milestone you achieve along the way.

- **Accept uncertainty**: Remember that every change involves risks but also offers growth opportunities.

- **Maintain a positive mindset**: Focus on the possibilities your new career can provide rather than the obstacles.

7. Evaluate and Adapt Your Path

As you navigate your career change, it's essential to remain flexible and open to new possibilities. Regularly evaluate your progress and ask yourself:

- Am I learning something new and meaningful?
- Is this path bringing me closer to my Ikigai?
- Are there adjustments I need to make to my plan?

Being adaptable allows you to face challenges with greater resilience and seize opportunities that may not have been evident initially.

Conclusion

Changing careers to follow your Ikigai is a transformative process that requires reflection, experimentation, and planning. By taking small, intentional steps and seeking support from others, you can align your professional life with your passions, talents, and values. While the journey may be challenging, the reward of living a life in harmony with your purpose is worth the effort.

Finding Balance Between Work and Personal Life in Harmony

The journey to discovering your **Ikigai** involves achieving a life of balance, where work serves as a source of meaning but not the sole focus of your existence. Often, professional demands consume so much of our energy that we neglect other critical areas of life, such as relationships, health, and leisure. Striking a balance between work and personal life not only promotes a healthier and more fulfilling existence but also brings you closer to your Ikigai, harmonizing what you do with who you are.

1. Recognize the Importance of Balance

The first step in achieving work-life balance is understanding that success is not measured solely by professional achievements. A fulfilling career is essential, but it's equally important to devote time and energy to other vital areas of life:

- **Personal relationships**: Building and maintaining meaningful connections with family, friends, and partners.

- **Physical well-being**: Taking care of your body through proper nutrition, exercise, and rest.

- **Personal growth**: Cultivating interests and passions outside of work.

- **Mental well-being**: Reducing stress and dedicating time to reflection and mindfulness.

Ask yourself, "Am I dedicating enough time to things that make me happy outside of work?" If the answer is no, it's time to make some adjustments.

2. Set Clear Boundaries Between Work and Personal Life

One of the primary reasons work can spill over into personal life is the lack of clear boundaries. Establishing these limits helps protect your time and create space for yourself and the people you care about. Here are some practical strategies:

- **Set defined work hours**: Decide when your workday starts and ends, and stick to it. Avoid checking emails or taking calls outside these hours unless absolutely necessary.

- **Create a dedicated workspace**: If you work from home, set up a specific area for work activities to maintain a physical distinction between work and personal spaces.

- **Learn to say no**: Don't automatically agree to every work request or commitment. Evaluate whether it's necessary and aligns with your goals.

For example, if a colleague asks you to work on a weekend project, assess its urgency and the impact on your personal time before agreeing.

3. Integrate Your Passions Into Daily Life

Balancing work and personal life doesn't necessarily mean separating the two completely. Sometimes, you can find harmony by integrating your passions into your work or dedicating time to activities you love outside the office.

For instance:

- If you love writing, you could start a blog or personal journal as a creative hobby.

- If you're passionate about music, set aside one evening a week to play an instrument or attend a concert.

- If your job lacks elements that excite you, look for ways to incorporate them into your day, even in small ways.

Spending time on activities that energize and inspire you helps maintain a positive perspective and recharge your energy.

4. Organize Your Time Strategically

Effective time management is essential for balancing work and personal life. Planning your day and week allows you to prioritize what truly matters without feeling overwhelmed.

Here are some useful techniques:

- **Block time for important activities**: Dedicate specific moments of your day to priorities like family time, exercise, or reading.

- **Simplify commitments**: Avoid overloading your schedule with too many activities. Focus on what is genuinely important.

- **Plan rest periods**: Ensure you have enough downtime to relax and recharge, avoiding overcommitment.

For example, you might choose to spend weekend mornings with your family, afternoons pursuing a personal hobby, and evenings resting.

5. Cultivate Meaningful Relationships

Relationships are a fundamental part of your Ikigai. Spending time with people who matter not only enriches your life but also provides a support network during challenging times. Here are some ideas to nurture meaningful relationships:

- Host weekly dinners with friends or family.
- Dedicate time daily to authentic conversations, free from distractions like phones.
- Join groups or communities that share your interests and values.

These moments of connection help you feel part of something larger and create a balance between work and personal life.

6. Recognize the Signs of Imbalance

Even with the best intentions, it's easy to fall into the trap of work overload. Recognizing signs of imbalance is the first step toward correcting course. Common signs include:

- Constant fatigue or stress.
- Little time for activities or people you love.
- Losing interest or enthusiasm for work or personal life.

If you notice these signs, take time to reflect and make adjustments to your routine.

Conclusion

Balancing work and personal life is an essential component of living according to your Ikigai. By setting clear boundaries, integrating your passions into daily life, and dedicating time to relationships and rest, you can create a more balanced and meaningful existence.

Remember, your Ikigai isn't just what you do for work—it's the harmony between all dimensions of your life. With intentional effort, you can find the right balance and live a fulfilling, satisfying life.

Capitolo 9
Ikigai and Relationships

"Wherever there is space between us, it is the place to build a bridge."

— Dzigar Kongtrul Rinpoche —

Building Meaningful Relationships Based on Your Values

Relationships are a fundamental part of Ikigai. While Ikigai is often seen as a personal journey, authentic and deep connections with others play a crucial role in living a meaningful and fulfilling life. Building relationships that reflect your values allows you to feel understood, supported, and motivated on your path. In this chapter, we explore how to identify your values, connect with others authentically, and cultivate meaningful relationships that enrich your life.

1. Understanding Your Core Values

Before building relationships based on your values, it's essential to know what those values are. Values are the guiding principles that define what is important to you in life. These might include honesty, kindness, personal growth, family, sustainability, creativity, and more.

Ask yourself:

- What principles guide my daily choices?
- What traits do I value most in the people I connect with?
- What makes me feel comfortable and in harmony with others?

For example, if you value authenticity, you might find relationships more fulfilling where people feel free to be themselves without fear of judgment.

Writing a list of your core values can help you clarify what to seek and nurture in your relationships.

2. Authentic Connections: The Foundation of Meaningful Relationships

Authentic relationships are built on genuine and sincere interactions. They are not just about sharing common interests but also about being truly present for each other. To create deep connections:

- **Be Authentic**: Don't be afraid to show who you truly are. Vulnerability often serves as the starting point for building trust and mutual understanding.

- **Practice Active Listening**: Give genuine attention and interest to the people you interact with. Avoid interruptions and show empathy for their feelings and perspectives.

- **Share Your Values**: Communicate your principles and life approach openly. This helps create common ground and establishes relationships on solid foundations.

For example, if one of your values is sustainability, you might seek connections with people who share your passion for the environment, perhaps through local groups or events dedicated to ecological causes.

3. Cultivating Relationships Through Intentional Actions

Meaningful relationships don't happen by chance; they require time, effort, and intention. Here are some strategies to strengthen bonds with people who share your values:

- **Spend Quality Time**: It's not about the quantity of time spent together but the quality. For instance, organize a dinner, a walk, or an activity that encourages deep and authentic conversations.

- **Show Gratitude**: Express appreciation for the people in your life. A simple "thank you" or a note of gratitude can strengthen bonds.

- **Support Your Friends and Family**: Be present in times of need, offering listening and help without expecting anything in return. Strong relationships often thrive on mutual support.

For example, offering your time to help a friend with a personal project or listening to them during a challenging time shows that you care about them.

4. Building Relationships Based on Shared Values

One of the most effective ways to create meaningful relationships is to seek people who share your core values. This doesn't mean limiting yourself to people identical to you but finding common ground to build a connection.

To do this:

- **Join Local Communities and Groups**: Look for events, workshops, or associations that reflect your interests and values. For example, if you love art, join painting classes or attend local exhibitions.

- **Use Digital Platforms Intentionally**: Participate in online groups or forums dedicated to topics you are passionate about. This allows you to connect with like-minded people, even outside your geographical area.

- **Create New Opportunities for Connection**: If you can't find existing groups that reflect your values, consider creating one. For example, you could organize a book club, a fundraiser for an important cause, or regular meetups with people who share your interests.

5. Overcoming Challenges in Relationships

Even the most meaningful relationships can encounter obstacles. Differences of opinion, misunderstandings, or personal changes can test a bond. To face these challenges:

- Communicate Openly: Express your feelings and listen to the other person's perspective without judgment.

- Find Compromise: Look for solutions that respect both your needs and values.

- Evaluate the Quality of the Bond: Not all relationships are meant to last forever. If a connection doesn't respect your values or makes you feel inauthentic, it might be time to let it go.

6. The Role of Relationships in Ikigai

Meaningful relationships enrich your life and support your Ikigai in several ways:

- **Provide Emotional Support**: Helping you overcome tough times and celebrate successes.

- **Stimulate Personal Growth**: People who share your values can inspire and motivate you to pursue your goals.

- **Create a Sense of Belonging**: Being part of a network of authentic relationships makes you feel connected to something greater.

For example, having friends who encourage your passions or colleagues who support your work can boost your sense of purpose and motivation.

Conclusion

Building meaningful relationships based on your values is a cornerstone of living according to your Ikigai. These connections not only provide support and motivation but also deeply enrich your life, helping you find balance and fulfillment. Through authenticity, intention, and effort, you can create a network of relationships that reflect your values and nurture your greater purpose.

How Ikigai Influences Your Connection with Others

Ikigai, understood as your personal purpose and reason for being, not only guides your individual journey but also profoundly shapes how you connect with those around you. Meaningful relationships are essential for living a fulfilling and rich life, and your Ikigai can serve as a compass to guide these connections. When you are aware of your purpose, you can build authentic relationships, communicate with greater empathy, and create bonds that reflect your deepest values.

1. Ikigai as a Foundation for Authentic Relationships

Knowing your Ikigai helps you understand who you truly are and what your priorities in life are. This awareness not only guides your personal path but also influences the type of relationships you build. When you are aligned with your purpose, you naturally surround yourself with people who share your values and aspirations, while distancing yourself from connections that do not reflect what truly matters to you.

For example, if your Ikigai is rooted in creativity and artistic expression, you may find great joy in connecting with people who share an interest in art or music. Attending exhibitions, painting workshops, or music groups can lead to relationships with individuals who understand and support your love for the arts. These connections not only enrich your personal life but also provide opportunities to grow and learn through meaningful exchanges.

Similarly, if your purpose is linked to improving human relationships, such as supporting local communities or helping those in need, you may find satisfaction in connecting with like-minded individuals. You could collaborate with groups organizing social events or inclusion projects, building relationships around shared goals and values.

These authentic connections improve the quality of your social life and offer a profound sense of belonging. When your relationships are built around shared Ikigai, they become a source of mutual inspiration and support.

Living according to your Ikigai also allows you to be more selective about the relationships you cultivate. This doesn't mean isolating yourself but rather choosing to dedicate your time and energy to people who enrich your life and push you toward your purpose. For example, you may prefer spending time with colleagues who value teamwork and collaboration rather than those who seek only competition or conflict.

2. The Role of Empathy and Listening

One of the most powerful effects of Ikigai is the ability to develop empathy in relationships. When you live in harmony with your purpose, you are more inclined to understand and respect the paths of others. This approach creates a space for authentic and deep listening, strengthening bonds and promoting open and sincere communication.

Practicing empathy means:

- Actively listening to what the other person has to say without interrupting or judging.

- Putting yourself in the other person's shoes to better understand their emotions and perspective.

- Offering support and understanding, even when you don't share the same experiences.

For example, if a friend shares a challenge related to work or family, your awareness of your Ikigai enables you to respond with sensitivity and respect, offering support that reflects your values.

3. Ikigai as an Inspiration for Others

Living according to your Ikigai not only enriches your life but can also inspire those around you. When you act with passion, authenticity, and purpose, you become a positive example for others, encouraging them to reflect on their own goals and values.

For instance:

- An entrepreneur who follows their Ikigai by creating an ethical and sustainable business may inspire colleagues and collaborators to make more conscious choices.

- A teacher who finds joy in educating their students not only imparts knowledge but also enthusiasm and passion, motivating others to give their best.

This ripple effect shows how Ikigai is not just an individual journey but a catalyst for positive change in others' lives.

4. Building Relationships That Support Your Ikigai

Meaningful relationships go beyond providing companionship; they can also offer support and encouragement for pursuing your Ikigai. Surrounding yourself with people who believe in you and your purpose helps you stay motivated and overcome challenges.

To build such relationships:

- **Share Your Ikigai**: Talk openly about your passions and goals with friends, family, and colleagues. This helps create a support network for your journey.

- **Seek Allies**: Find people who share similar interests or are willing to collaborate with you on meaningful projects.

- **Ask for and Offer Support**: Don't hesitate to ask for help when you need it, and be ready to do the same for others.

For example, if your Ikigai involves writing, you could join a writers' group to share ideas, receive feedback, and find inspiration.

5. Overcoming Relationship Challenges with Ikigai

Even the most meaningful relationships can face challenges. Ikigai provides a point of reference for navigating these difficulties, helping you remain true to your values and manage conflicts constructively.

To overcome relational difficulties:

- **Communicate Authentically**: Express your feelings and needs clearly and respectfully, avoiding the temptation to hide your thoughts.

- **Recognize Differences**: Not everyone you interact with will share your Ikigai. Accept these differences and seek common ground.

- **Evaluate the Relationship**: If a connection doesn't respect your values or pulls you away from your purpose, it may be necessary to reassess the relationship.

6. Ikigai and the Sense of Belonging

One of the most rewarding aspects of Ikigai is the sense of belonging that comes from connecting with others. When you live according to your purpose, you not only feel more personally fulfilled but also contribute to creating a community of people who share similar values.

For example, a volunteer working for a social cause finds not only satisfaction in their efforts but also a sense of belonging to a network of people striving for a common goal.

Conclusion

Ikigai profoundly influences how you connect with others, fostering more authentic, empathetic, and meaningful relationships. By living according to your purpose, you not only enhance the quality of your connections but also inspire others to do the same. Cultivating these relationships is not just a way to enrich your life but also a means of contributing to a more harmonious and interconnected world.

Finding Inspiration and Support in the Community

Community plays a crucial role in discovering and strengthening your Ikigai. Humans are not meant to live in isolation; our purpose often emerges, grows, and solidifies through interactions with others. A community—understood as a group of people sharing values, goals, or interests—is not only a place of belonging but also a source of inspiration and a pillar of support during challenging times. This chapter explores how to identify, build, and nurture communal bonds that enrich your journey toward Ikigai.

1. Why Community Is Essential for Ikigai

A community is much more than a collection of people; it is an environment that provides support, encouragement, and a sense of belonging. Being part of a group that shares similar interests or values reinforces your identity and helps you feel connected to something larger. This connection is particularly vital when facing challenges or moments of uncertainty on your journey.

Example:

A person whose Ikigai involves caregiving may draw strength and energy from a support group for caregivers, where they can share experiences, receive practical advice, and find solace among people who understand their challenges.

2. Identifying the Right Community for You

Not all communities will align with your Ikigai. It's important to find groups or environments that reflect your values and aspirations. To identify the right community, consider:

- **Your Interests**: What are your passions or favorite activities? Look for groups or associations related to these themes.

- **Your Values**: Spend time with people who respect and promote the principles you hold dear.
- **Your Goals**: If your Ikigai involves a specific project, such as starting a business or improving a skill, seek out communities that can offer support and resources in that area.

Example:

If you love literature, join a local book club or attend literary events where you can connect with people who share your passion for reading.

3. Community as a Source of Inspiration

Being part of a community isn't just about receiving support—it's also about finding inspiration through the experiences, stories, and successes of others. Communities offer a unique opportunity for mutual learning, where you can discover new perspectives and ideas.

Examples:

- An aspiring entrepreneur might draw inspiration from a group of professionals sharing their success stories and challenges.
- A musician participating in jam sessions with other artists might find fresh ideas for compositions.
- A teacher joining a network of educators might learn innovative approaches to engaging their students.

Interacting with people pursuing their dreams encourages you to reflect on your journey and find new motivation to achieve your goals.

4. Creating Relationships of Mutual Support

Authentic communities thrive on give-and-take. It's not just about seeking support but also about offering your contributions. Actively participating in a community strengthens bonds and creates a positive and motivating environment.

Strategies for Building Mutually Supportive Relationships:

- **Participate Actively:** Don't just be a passive observer. Offer your time, skills, and energy to help others.

- **Share Your Experiences:** Talk about your journey and successes—your story might inspire someone facing similar challenges.

- **Ask for Help When Needed:** Showing vulnerability and seeking support is a sign of strength. People are often more willing to help than we realize.

Example:

If you're part of a volunteer group, you might propose a specific project or help organize an event. These small actions strengthen connections and make you feel like an integral part of the community.

5. Building a Community If You Can't Find One

If you can't find a community that aligns with your Ikigai, consider creating one. Organizing a group, event, or social network around your interests and values not only connects you with like-minded people but can also become an essential part of your Ikigai.

Examples:

- If you love cooking, organize a monthly culinary night with friends and acquaintances.

- If your Ikigai is tied to art, start an open creative workshop.

- If you're interested in personal growth, create a discussion group centered around motivational books or themes.

Such initiatives not only enrich your life but also provide a meaningful contribution to others.

6. Community in Times of Difficulty

Community becomes especially important during times of crisis or change. Being surrounded by people who support and believe in you can make the difference between feeling overwhelmed and finding the strength to move forward. Authentic communities offer a safe space where you can share concerns, receive advice, and find comfort.

Example:

A trusted group of friends or a professional network can help you navigate the loss of a job by providing opportunities, ideas, and encouragement. Knowing you're not alone during tough times is one of the greatest benefits of being part of a community.

Conclusion

Finding inspiration and support in the community is a fundamental aspect of your journey toward Ikigai. Authentic connections not only help you grow as an individual but also offer a support network to accompany you through challenges and celebrate your successes. Actively participating in a community—or creating one if needed—enriches your experience and brings you closer to your purpose, making your journey even more meaningful.

How Ikigai Can Help You During Difficult Times

Moments of crisis—whether tied to a loss, an unexpected change, or a sense of confusion—are inevitable in life. During these phases, it is easy to feel overwhelmed, directionless, and drained of energy to move forward. It is precisely in such moments that Ikigai can become an inner compass, offering stability, strength, and motivation to face challenges. Ikigai is not just a philosophy for peaceful days; it is a profound anchor that helps you navigate personal storms and rediscover a sense of purpose, even in adversity.

1. Finding a Point of Reference in Chaos

When life feels unbalanced, Ikigai offers a point of reference. Your Ikigai represents what is most important to you: your passions, talents, values, and contributions to the world. Even during difficult times, these elements remain constant. Reflecting on what gives your life meaning helps you focus on what you can still control, rather than being swept away by chaos.

For example, a person whose Ikigai is helping others can concentrate on small acts of kindness, like assisting a neighbor or listening to a friend in need, thereby rediscovering a sense of purpose even in uncertain times.

2. Focusing on Small, Meaningful Actions

In a crisis, it's easy to feel overwhelmed by the weight of challenges and forget the value of small steps. Ikigai encourages you to focus on daily actions that reflect your purpose and help you maintain a positive perspective. Even small gestures can make a difference—for both yourself and those around you.

Examples:

- If your Ikigai is tied to creativity, dedicating just 10 minutes a day to painting, writing, or playing an instrument can bring relief and a sense of continuity.

- If your purpose involves nurturing relationships, making a call to a friend or arranging a meetup can remind you of the importance of human connections.

These actions, no matter how small, help keep your Ikigai alive even in the toughest times.

3. Building Resilience Through Your Ikigai

Resilience is the ability to face challenges with strength and adaptability. Ikigai helps you build resilience by giving you a reason to keep going, even when everything seems to be falling apart. Knowing you have a larger purpose gives you the courage to confront challenges with a positive mindset. For example, the elderly in Okinawa, known for their longevity and serenity, attribute part of their resilience to their Ikigai. Even in times of loss or economic hardship, they find motivation in activities like tending a garden, preserving traditions, or caring for their family. This approach not only helps them overcome crises but also strengthens their ability to find joy in the small things.

4. The Power of Gratitude and Mindfulness

In difficult moments, it's common to focus on what's missing or what's gone wrong. Ikigai instead invites you to focus on what you still have and what gives you strength. Cultivating gratitude helps shift your attention from difficulties to the resources around you.

Practices to Adopt:

- **Gratitude Journal**: Each day, write down three things you are grateful for. These can be simple things like a warm meal or a smile from a stranger.

- **Mindfulness Practice**: Spend a few minutes meditating or reflecting to stay present and avoid being overwhelmed by worries.

For example, someone facing a work crisis might focus on the support they receive from family or the opportunity to learn new skills, finding strength to move forward.

5. Building a Support Network Around Your Ikigai

A crisis does not have to be faced alone. Your Ikigai not only connects you to yourself but can also help you build a support network. Meaningful relationships, based on shared values, can provide comfort and encouragement during tough times.

Examples:

- If your Ikigai is connected to nature exploration, you could find support and inspiration in hiking groups, conservation associations, or communities dedicated to exploring landscapes. Through these connections, you might discover new trails, deepen your knowledge of biodiversity, and share experiences that fuel your passion for adventure and respect for the environment.

- If your purpose is linked to physical well-being, join groups promoting sports activities or mindfulness practices. Sharing your Ikigai with others helps you feel less isolated and more understood.

6. Finding Meaning Even in Challenges

Finally, Ikigai encourages you to view moments of crisis not just as obstacles but also as opportunities for growth. Every difficulty can teach you something new about yourself and the world around you. Even in the hardest challenges, your Ikigai can guide you toward a deeper understanding of your journey. For instance, a personal loss might lead you to rediscover the importance of relationships and invest more time in caring for loved ones. Similarly, a professional setback could push you to explore new opportunities and redefine your priorities.

Conclusion

Ikigai is not just a guide for peaceful moments but a valuable resource for facing crises with strength and awareness. Recognizing your purpose and acting in alignment with it helps you overcome difficulties, regain balance, and discover new meanings even in the darkest moments. By cultivating your Ikigai, you can transform challenges into opportunities and continue to live a life rich in meaning and fulfillment.

Facing Burnout, Stress, and Uncertainty

Stress, burnout, and uncertainty are common challenges in modern life, driven by fast-paced routines, high expectations, and a constantly changing world. These emotional states can leave you feeling overwhelmed, drained of energy, and disconnected from your purpose. Ikigai, as a philosophy of life, offers practical tools and a holistic approach to navigating these tough times, helping you regain balance, motivation, and serenity.Understanding the Causes of Burnout and Stress.The first step in overcoming burnout and stress is identifying their root causes. Often, these emotional states arise from a combination of factors that, when compounded, lead to a sense of overwhelm and disconnection from your Ikigai. Recognizing what triggers these feelings allows you to address them consciously and regain control.

1. Work Overload

One of the main contributors to stress and burnout is work overload. Constant pressure to meet deadlines, achieve goals, or meet high expectations can lead to mental and physical exhaustion.

This often occurs when:

- **No clear boundaries are set**: For example, responding to emails outside of work hours or taking on too many responsibilities without delegating.

- **No restorative breaks are taken**: Working for long periods without adequate rest or vacations.

- **Demands exceed resources**: Facing workloads that require more time, energy, or skills than you have available.

For instance, a project manager juggling multiple projects without adequate support might feel perpetually behind and unsatisfied with their outcomes.

2. Lack of Meaning

Another common cause of burnout is a sense of meaninglessness. When your daily activities do not align with your values or Ikigai, it's easy to feel unfulfilled and demotivated.

This happens, for example, when:

- You work in a role you're not passionate about, just to earn a paycheck.

- You engage in tasks that feel repetitive or purposeless, without any visible positive impact.

- You feel disconnected from the final outcome of your work or fail to see how your contribution matters.

For example, a graphic designer working on purely commercial projects with no room for creativity might feel empty and alienated, even if the job pays well.

3. Uncertainty About the Future

Fear of the unknown is another significant source of stress. Not knowing what the future holds, whether you're making the right decisions, or how to handle unforeseen events can create anxiety and emotional blocks.

This type of stress often arises in situations like:

- **Sudden changes**: Such as losing a job, relocating, or experiencing a major life transition.

- **Chronic indecision**: Struggling to make decisions out of fear of making the wrong choice.

- **External pressure**: Feeling obligated to follow paths dictated by others' expectations rather than your aspirations.

A common example is a recent graduate feeling overwhelmed by the fear of not finding a fulfilling job or choosing a career path that doesn't suit them.

Acknowledging These Dynamics

Recognizing the causes of stress and burnout is the first step in addressing them. Identifying what drains your energy or leaves you feeling dissatisfied enables you to take conscious steps to change the situation. Track moments when you feel overwhelmed and try to understand the activities, contexts, or emotions underlying those states. Only by deeply understanding these dynamics can you begin to restore balance and reconnect with your Ikigai.

2. Using Ikigai as a Compass to Rebalance

Ikigai invites you to reconsider your priorities and focus on what energizes and gives you meaning. During times of stress or burnout, it can help you:

- **Reconnect with what you love to do**: Spend time on activities that bring you joy, even if only for a few minutes a day. This can help recharge your energy and reduce stress.

- **Leverage your skills**: Concentrating on what you excel at can provide a sense of accomplishment and confidence.

- **Reflect on the world's needs**: Thinking about how you can contribute to others, even in simple ways, can restore purpose to your actions.

For example, someone whose Ikigai lies in storytelling could spend time writing, either for themselves or to share with others, as a way to find peace and purpose.

3. Practicing Mindfulness to Manage Stress

Mindfulness is a powerful tool for addressing stress and burnout. Being present in the moment helps prevent you from being overwhelmed by future worries or past regrets. To incorporate mindfulness into your routine:

- **Meditate daily**: Even 5-10 minutes of meditation can reduce anxiety and improve your ability to face challenges.

- **Be mindful in daily activities**: Focus on the present moment while eating, walking, or working. This simple act can lower stress and increase your connection with what you're doing.

- **Practice mindful breathing**: When feeling overwhelmed, pause and focus on your breath. Take deep breaths in and exhale slowly, releasing tension.

For instance, a professional feeling swamped by deadlines could take a brief pause for deep breathing, regaining the calm needed to tackle responsibilities.

4. Building a Support Network

No one should face stress or burnout alone. Connecting with others is an essential part of your Ikigai and can provide crucial emotional support during tough times. To build a support network:

- **Share your feelings**: Talking with friends, family, or colleagues about what you're going through can relieve pressure and help you feel understood.

- **Seek like-minded communities**: Join groups or associations that share your interests or purpose. These connections can strengthen and inspire you.

- **Don't hesitate to seek professional help**: If stress or burnout becomes unmanageable, consider reaching out to a therapist or coach who can guide you on your journey.

For example, a hiking enthusiast might join a local trekking group, finding strength and motivation through connection with fellow nature lovers.

5. Reorganizing Your Priorities

One of the most important steps in combating burnout is reorganizing your priorities. Overload often stems from trying to do too much or meet unrealistic expectations. Ikigai helps you distinguish between what is essential and what can be let go.

Steps to Take:

- **Set boundaries**: Learn to say no to tasks or commitments that don't align with your Ikigai.

- **Create a balanced routine**: Allocate time not just for work, but also for rest, relationships, and activities you love.

- **Do one thing at a time**: Avoid multitasking, which can increase stress. Focus on completing one task before moving to the next.

For example, a freelancer feeling overwhelmed might reduce their client load and focus on projects they are truly passionate about.

6. Finding Meaning in Difficulties

Ikigai teaches you that even challenges can be a source of learning and growth. When going through a crisis, ask yourself:

- What can I learn from this experience?
- How can I turn this challenge into an opportunity for growth?

For instance, someone who has lost their job might discover new passions or skills during the transition, finding a renewed purpose in their career.

Conclusion

Facing burnout, stress, and uncertainty is never easy, but with the guidance of Ikigai, these challenging moments can be transformed into opportunities for reflection, growth, and renewed purpose. By focusing on what truly matters to you, practicing mindfulness, and building a support network, you can restore balance and serenity. Remember, your Ikigai is always present, ready to guide you through even the toughest storms, offering strength and motivation to move forward.

Rediscovering Your Purpose After Failure or Major Change

Failure or sudden change can deeply shake your sense of purpose and direction in life. Whether it's job loss, a separation, a personal crisis, or a change that disrupts your routine, it's normal to feel disoriented, discouraged, and, at times, disconnected from your Ikigai. However, these moments, when approached with awareness, can become opportunities to reevaluate your priorities and redefine your purpose. With its holistic approach, Ikigai provides a practical and reflective framework to regain balance, strength, and a renewed sense of direction.

1. Accepting Failure as Part of the Journey

The first step to rediscovering your Ikigai after failure or change is to accept what has happened. Often, failure is seen as an endpoint, but it can actually be a valuable lesson.

Accepting that every journey has its ups and downs allows you to look forward with greater openness.

Helpful Reflections:

- **Reassess the meaning of failure**: View it not as a defeat but as an opportunity to learn and grow. Every mistake holds lessons that can enrich your journey.

- **Cultivate resilience**: Remember that failure doesn't define who you are—it's only a temporary phase. Focus on the resources you have to move forward.

For instance, an entrepreneur who experienced a business failure might reflect on what they learned from the experience, such as new skills gained, mistakes to avoid in the future, and new opportunities that have emerged.

2. Exploring What Truly Motivates You

Failure or a major change often signals that your previous path may not have been fully aligned with your Ikigai. Use this opportunity to reflect on what truly motivates you.

Questions to Consider:

- What makes me feel alive and fulfilled?
- Which activities or experiences have brought me the most satisfaction in the past?
- What are my core values, and how can I live them in my daily life?

For example, someone who has lost their job might realize they weren't genuinely satisfied with their previous career and that it's time to explore new paths, such as pursuing a creative endeavor or a project aligned with their values.

3. Reconnecting with the Four Pillars of Ikigai

A crisis is an opportunity to reevaluate the four pillars of Ikigai and recalibrate your life. Here's how to work on each pillar:

- **What you love to do:** Identify activities that excite you and make you feel fulfilled. Spend time on these passions, even in small and gradual ways.

- **What you are good at:** Reflect on your skills and talents. Consider how you can use them in new or creative ways to address your situation.

- **What the world needs:** Think about how your abilities and passions can address a real need. Helping others often restores a sense of purpose.

- **What you can be paid for:** Explore new professional opportunities that allow you to combine your passions and skills with a source of income.

For example, a teacher who has left their job might explore new ways to share knowledge, such as organizing workshops, creating online courses, or collaborating with nontraditional educational organizations.

4. Experimenting with New Directions

A significant change can be the perfect time to try new activities and discover aspects of yourself you've never explored. Experimentation broadens your horizons without requiring an immediate, definitive commitment.

Ideas to Begin:

- **Take courses or workshops:** Discover new interests and skills that might be key to your future.

- **Collaborate with others:** Join projects or initiatives that let you explore different fields.

- **Start a personal project:** Dedicate time to a hobby or idea you've always wanted to pursue, even just for the joy of it.

For example, someone who left the corporate world might decide to explore photography, design, or social activism to see which new direction resonates most.

5. Finding Support Through Relationships

Meaningful relationships can be a critical resource during times of crisis. Sharing your thoughts and feelings with friends, family, or mentors can help you clarify your ideas and regain strength.

How to Leverage Others' Support:

- **Seek advice**: Those who know you well can offer new perspectives and helpful suggestions.

- **Join a community**: Participate in groups or associations related to your interests. These connections can inspire you and foster meaningful relationships.

- **Nurture quality relationships**: Spend time strengthening bonds with people who support and share your values.

For instance, an avid hiker could join a local trekking group, finding not only a sense of belonging but also new ideas for transforming their passion into a meaningful project.

6. Turning Change into Opportunity

A failure or a change is not an end but a new beginning. Ikigai helps you see these moments as opportunities to grow and reinvent yourself. Ask yourself:

- What can I learn from this experience?

- What new possibilities are opening up for me?

- How can I use this crisis to move closer to my Ikigai?

For example, someone who has gone through a separation might choose to dedicate more time to themselves, exploring new passions or strengthening relationships they had previously neglected.

Conclusion

Rediscovering your purpose after a failure or significant change requires time, reflection, and action. Ikigai provides a compass to navigate these moments, helping you reconnect with what truly matters and transform challenges into opportunities. Through acceptance, experimentation, and the support of meaningful relationships, you can rebuild your sense of purpose and embark on an even richer and more fulfilling journey.

Real-Life Stories of People Who Found Their Ikigai

Ikigai is not just an abstract concept but a practical philosophy that has transformed many lives. Real-life stories of those who have found their Ikigai demonstrate how one can live a meaningful life, overcome obstacles, and achieve balance. In this chapter, we will explore testimonies from individuals who, by following their purpose, discovered not only a clear direction for their existence but also a profound connection with themselves and others.

1. Keiko's Story: An Artisan Rediscovering Tradition

Keiko, a 42-year-old woman living in a small town in Kyoto Prefecture, Japan, had worked for over a decade in a tech company. Despite her well-paid job, she felt unfulfilled. The work neither reflected her values nor her passion for traditional crafts—a love she had developed in her youth while watching her grandmother weave handmade kimonos. Tired of the corporate grind, Keiko decided to take a sabbatical year to rediscover herself. During this time, she returned to her hometown and relearned the art of traditional weaving. She found that working with her hands, creating unique pieces, and preserving local culture made her feel alive. Soon, she began sharing her creations on social media and selling her kimonos to a niche market interested in tradition. Keiko found her Ikigai in the intersection of passion, vocation, mission, and profession. She not only creates high-quality garments but also conducts workshops to teach younger generations the importance of preserving traditional craftsmanship. "It's not just a job," Keiko says, "it's my way of keeping my homeland's cultural roots alive."

2. Marco's Renewal: From Engineering to Environmental Volunteering

Marco, a 35-year-old engineer from Milan, had a promising career at a major construction company. Yet, he felt increasing discomfort about the environmental impact of the projects he worked on. While technically stimulating, the work clashed with his growing environmental concerns. A vacation trip to the Amazon changed his perspective. There, Marco joined a local group engaged in reforestation and biodiversity preservation. Planting trees and working with local communities made him feel, for the first time, deeply connected to a sense of purpose. Upon returning home, Marco made a bold decision: he left his job to dedicate himself to environmental volunteering. After a few months, Marco began collaborating with an NGO, using his engineering skills to develop sustainable solutions for conservation projects. Now, Marco lives his Ikigai by protecting the planet, merging his technical expertise with his personal mission. "I've found work that not only excites me but also creates a positive impact," he shares.

3. Sofia: A Young Chef Turning Passion into Inclusive Careers

Sofia, a 28-year-old chef from Barcelona, always loved cooking. As a child, she spent hours in the kitchen with her mother, experimenting with flavors and creating original recipes. However, when she started working in fine dining, she realized the culinary world was competitive and often lacked empathy. Determined to do something different, Sofia decided to combine her love for cooking with her desire to create positive social impact. She opened a small bistro that not only served innovative and delicious dishes but also provided job opportunities for individuals facing barriers to employment, such as people with disabilities or refugees. Her restaurant quickly became a welcoming space where every dish told a story, and every worker felt valued. Today, Sofia is an example of how Ikigai can be found at the intersection of passion and mission. "Every day, I'm not just cooking," she says, "but creating a space where my team and customers feel inspired and embraced."

4. Ahmed's Journey: A Photographer Capturing Stories of Hope

Ahmed, originally from Marrakech, was a professional photographer specializing in events. However, he found his work repetitive and felt it did not allow him to express his true talent. During a trip to West Africa, Ahmed was moved by the stories of local communities facing challenges like drought and poverty but demonstrating extraordinary resilience. He decided to dedicate his work to visually narrating stories of hope and resilience. His photographs, which depict not only hardship but also the strength of the people, began appearing in international magazines and were exhibited in galleries. Ahmed now uses his talent to raise awareness about social injustices and to fundraise for the communities he photographs. Ahmed found his Ikigai by turning his creative passion into a tool for change. "Photography is not just an art for me," he explains, "it's a way to build bridges between cultures and tell stories that truly matter."

Conclusion

These stories show that finding your Ikigai is a unique and personal journey. Whether it's preserving tradition, protecting the environment, promoting inclusivity, or sharing stories through art, the common thread is the ability to unite passions, talents, the world's needs, and personal vision.Ikigai is not something discovered overnight; it's an ongoing journey that enriches both your life and the lives of others. These testimonies serve as inspiration and a reminder that a sense of purpose is always within reach if we have the courage to listen to and follow it.

The Experience of Okinawa's Residents: Living to 100 in Harmony

The island of Okinawa, Japan, is known as one of the world's "blue zones"—regions where people live longer and healthier lives than the global average. The residents of Okinawa frequently reach 100 years of age while maintaining high levels of physical, mental, and emotional well-being. At the heart of this extraordinary longevity lies the concept of Ikigai, a life philosophy that for Okinawans is not just a theory but a daily practice that brings meaning and purpose to their lives.

1. A Life Approach Based on Harmony

Okinawans live by a key principle: their Ikigai—the reason they wake up every morning—is deeply intertwined with their daily lives. Unlike many modern societies dominated by fast-paced routines and external pressures, Okinawans build their days around what they love to do, what they excel at, what the world needs, and how they can be useful. For many, Ikigai is not about achieving grand, long-term goals but embracing small joys and purposes that add value to life.

For instance, some find their Ikigai in tending their gardens, others in cooking for their families, and still others in passing down stories and traditions to younger generations. This approach helps them live in harmony with themselves and the world around them.

2. Social Connection: The Role of Moai

One distinctive feature of Okinawan culture is their strong social network. The islanders participate in groups called moai—small support communities created to provide emotional, practical, and financial assistance. These groups, often formed in youth, remain active throughout life, offering a sense of belonging and security.

Moai is not just a means of navigating difficulties but also a constant source of joy and motivation. Members regularly meet to share meals, tell stories, and support one another. This deep sense of social connection reduces stress and significantly contributes to emotional well-being, one of the key ingredients of their longevity.

For example, an elderly woman living alone might find companionship in her moai, whose members help her with small chores or share moments of leisure. These deep bonds go beyond practical aid, creating a network that strengthens resilience and a sense of purpose.

3. The Importance of a Balanced Lifestyle

Okinawans' longevity is not just the result of their mindset but also their daily habits. A balanced lifestyle, rooted in the principles of Ikigai, is an integral part of their lives.

- **Healthy Diet:** The Okinawan diet is renowned for being simple and balanced. Residents primarily consume fresh vegetables, legumes, tofu, and fish, while limiting red meat and processed foods. They also follow the principle of hara hachi bu, which advises eating until they are 80% full to avoid overeating.

- **Regular Physical Activity:** For Okinawans, physical activity is not an obligation but a natural part of their daily routine. They walk, tend to their gardens, and practice activities like tai chi, keeping their bodies active and healthy.

- **Slow Living:** Unlike modern societies that often prioritize productivity at the expense of well-being, Okinawans take time to appreciate small pleasures. They dedicate moments to reflection, gratitude, and rest, maintaining a balance between mind and body.

4. A Sense of Belonging to Traditions

Okinawa's cultural and spiritual traditions play a crucial role in giving life meaning. Many residents find their Ikigai in passing down knowledge, values, and stories to future generations. This process not only strengthens family bonds but also gives them a sense of continuity and purpose.

For instance, an elder might teach their grandchildren the art of traditional weaving or how to prepare local dishes, passing on not only practical skills but also a connection to their cultural identity. This sense of belonging to their history and community provides deep satisfaction and a reason to live enthusiastically, even in old age.

5. Ikigai as a Key Factor in Longevity

Okinawans demonstrate that the secret to longevity lies not only in genetics but also in their ability to live according to their Ikigai. This concept helps them find meaning in small things, maintain authentic relationships, and care for themselves and others.

For example, a study on Okinawa's centenarians found that most continue to engage in meaningful activities even in old age. Whether it's cultivating a garden, participating in community events, or caring for a family member, these activities give them a reason to wake up each morning with enthusiasm.

Conclusion

The experience of Okinawa's residents serves as a shining example of how Ikigai can be applied to everyday life to live longer and in harmony. Through a combination of social connection, a balanced lifestyle, and a positive approach to life, they manage to find happiness and meaning even in the simplest things. Their stories teach us that Ikigai is not something distant or unattainable, but a principle that anyone can embrace to enhance their quality of life.

How to Cultivate a Happier and More Balanced World with Ikigai

In a world increasingly characterized by fast-paced rhythms, social pressures, and growing disconnection among people, Ikigai offers a model for cultivating not just individual well-being, but also collective harmony. Living according to your Ikigai not only enriches your personal life but also contributes to building a happier, more balanced, and sustainable society. Ikigai, with its focus on balancing what you love, what you are good at, what the world needs, and what you can be paid for, serves as a philosophy that can guide positive change in communities and across the globe.

1. Spreading Ikigai in Personal Relationships

The first step to building a happier world is to live Ikigai in your daily relationships. When you nurture meaningful connections based on empathy, respect, and shared values, you inspire others to do the same. Ikigai, which encourages authenticity and harmony, helps foster deeper and more fulfilling bonds.

For example:

- **Sharing your purpose**: Speaking openly about your Ikigai with friends and family can inspire them to reflect on their journey and seek what gives meaning to their lives.

- **Practicing kindness**: Everyday actions like offering support, listening attentively, or giving sincere compliments can create a positive atmosphere and encourage similar behavior in others.

- **Creating spaces for dialogue**: Hosting gatherings or discussions that encourage people to explore their Ikigai can strengthen social connections and promote a sense of community.

For instance, a parent who finds their Ikigai in educating their children can inspire a family culture based on mutual respect and the appreciation of individual talents.

2 Integrating Ikigai into the Workplace

Creating a happier world also involves fostering healthier, more meaningful workplaces. Applying Ikigai principles at work can transform organizational dynamics, increasing employee satisfaction and productivity. When people work in alignment with their purpose, they feel more motivated and engaged.

Ways to apply Ikigai in professional settings:

- **Promoting employee well-being**: Companies can help their employees discover their Ikigai through personal development programs and workshops that encourage reflection on passions, skills, and values.

- **Creating inclusive work environments**: Workplaces that value diversity and provide opportunities to nurture unique talents foster a culture of belonging and collaboration.

- **Aligning personal and corporate purpose**: Leaders can connect company goals with the individual motivations of employees, creating a shared sense of mission.

For example, a sustainability-focused company could offer employees opportunities to participate in eco-friendly projects, integrating personal and collective values.

Driving Change in Local Communities

Ikigai can also be a transformative force in communities. When groups of people share a common purpose and work together to achieve it, strong bonds and lasting impacts are created. Communities that embrace Ikigai principles tend to be more resilient, collaborative, and content.

Practical ways to bring Ikigai into communities:

- **Promote local initiatives**: Organize events or projects that encourage community members to contribute their skills and passions, such as solidarity markets, volunteer groups, or creative workshops.

- **Create meeting spaces**: Establish physical or virtual spaces where people can share experiences, discuss ideas, and support one another.

- **Cultivate a sense of belonging**: Engage in projects that strengthen connections to the local area, such as environmental clean-ups, public space revitalization, or cultural celebrations.

For example, a small community might start an urban gardening project where participants cultivate not just food, but also relationships and a shared sense of purpose.

4. Inspiring Future Generations

A happier and more balanced world depends on how we educate the next generation. Teaching young people the principles of Ikigai from an early age helps them develop self-awareness, empathy, and the ability to contribute to collective well-being.

Ways to promote Ikigai among young people:

- **Experiential education:** Provide opportunities to explore interests and talents through hands-on activities, such as art, sports, or science workshops.

- **Mentoring and guidance:** Connect young people with mentors who can help them discover and nurture their Ikigai.

- **Encourage reflection:** Introduce tools like journals or group sessions to help youth explore their passions, skills, and values.

For instance, a school might introduce programs on sustainability or leadership, giving students opportunities to experiment with their potential and their impact on the world.

5. Ikigai as a Tool for Global Sustainability

Finally, Ikigai can play a vital role in building a more sustainable future for the planet. When people live according to their purpose, they are more likely to make mindful decisions and contribute to the greater good.

How Ikigai aligns with sustainability:

- **Conscious consumption:** Living in line with your Ikigai means avoiding waste and making purchases that reflect your values.

- **Participation in global initiatives:** Join movements that promote change, such as climate action or social justice campaigns.

- **Integrating sustainable values in businesses**: Companies guided by Ikigai tend to promote ethical and sustainable practices, contributing to a better world.

Conclusion

Cultivating a happier and more balanced world with Ikigai is possible if each of us begins to live according to our purpose and inspires others to do the same. Through personal relationships, work, local communities, and the education of future generations, we can create a more harmonious, resilient, and meaningful society. Ikigai is not just a tool for individual well-being but a vision for a better future, built step by step by each of us.

Applying Ikigai to Sustainability and Collective Well-being

A life based on Ikigai is deeply connected to the concept of contribution. When your passions and skills align with the needs of your community or environment, you create a balance that enriches not only your existence but also the world around you. This principle is especially relevant to sustainability, which requires an integrated and collaborative approach.

For example:

- A creative designer might use their skills to design sustainable products, such as furniture made from recycled materials.

- A passionate educator could launch programs to teach younger generations about the importance of environmental protection.

- A social entrepreneur might establish a company promoting circular economy practices, reducing waste, and maximizing resources.

The central idea is to discover your personal purpose and use it as a driving force to address collective needs.

2. Sustainability as a Global Need

Sustainability is not just an option; it is an urgent necessity to ensure a future for our planet. Issues such as climate change, biodiversity loss, and pollution are global challenges that require everyone's collaboration. Ikigai offers a practical framework to transform individual awareness into collective action.

Applying Ikigai to sustainability:

- **Reflect on what you love:** Engage in activities that excite you while contributing to environmental or social well-being, such as volunteering for ecological projects or promoting awareness campaigns.

- **Use your skills:** Identify your talents and think about how they can address sustainability challenges. For instance, a technology expert might develop solutions to reduce CO_2 emissions.

- **Address the planet's needs**: Reflect on specific issues, such as waste reduction or renewable energy promotion, within your sphere of influence.

3. Creating Impact Through Concrete Actions

Applying Ikigai to sustainability requires translating values and purpose into concrete actions. Small steps can make a big difference when adopted collectively.

Ideas to get started:

- **Reduce your personal ecological footprint**: Adopt more sustainable daily habits, such as conscious consumption, low-impact transportation, and waste reduction.

- **Join local projects:** Participate in groups or associations working to protect the environment in your community, such as beach cleanups or park restoration.

- **Support ethical businesses**: Choose to buy from companies that follow sustainable practices and respect workers' rights.

For instance, someone passionate about fashion could support ethical brands or create their own clothing line using eco-friendly fabrics and sustainable processes.

4. Educating and Inspiring Others

One of the most powerful aspects of applying Ikigai to sustainability is the potential to inspire others. Every individual living in harmony with their Ikigai and contributing to collective well-being can positively influence those around them.

Strategies to share your Ikigai:

- **Share knowledge**: Host workshops, conferences, or local events to educate your community on sustainability and collective well-being.

- **Create inspiring content**: Use social media or blogs to share your journey and encourage others to do the same.

- **Lead by example**: Demonstrate through your daily actions that it's possible to live sustainably without compromising quality of life.

For example, an architect integrating sustainable building practices into their projects not only reduces environmental impact but also shows clients and colleagues a different way of constructing.

5. Sustainability and Global Collaboration

The application of Ikigai to sustainability extends beyond individual or local levels and can contribute to global collaboration. The connection between individuals, communities, and nations is essential to address issues that transcend geographic boundaries.

How to contribute globally:

- **Join international movements**: Participate in global initiatives such as Fridays for Future or Plastic Free July to amplify your impact.

- **Collaborate with NGOs:** Work with non-governmental organizations promoting sustainable development projects worldwide.

- **Innovate for scale:** Use your Ikigai to develop solutions that can be implemented on a larger scale.

For example, an engineer passionate about renewable energy might collaborate with an NGO to bring solar energy solutions to rural communities without access to electricity.

6. A Sustainable Future Through Ikigai

Ikigai provides a vision to guide humanity toward a more sustainable and harmonious future. Living in line with your purpose means acting intentionally, with respect for the planet and others. As more people embrace this philosophy, a collective force emerges that can drive change. Sustainability, viewed through the lens of Ikigai, is not merely a sacrifice or obligation but an opportunity to build a world where people and the environment thrive together.

Conclusion

Applying Ikigai to sustainability and collective well-being is a choice that enriches both individual and global life. Through mindful actions, sharing, and collaboration, we can address today's challenges and build a more equitable and balanced future. Living according to Ikigai not only helps us find our purpose but also invites us to actively contribute to creating a better world, one small step at a time.

The Journey Toward Your Ikigai: A Unique and Personal Path

The journey to discover your Ikigai is a unique and personal process of exploration, reflection, and action. It's not a destination to reach once and for all, but a continuous path that evolves with you, adapting to life's changes. This process takes time and patience, but the benefits—balance, happiness, and a sense of purpose—make every step worthwhile and meaningful. Throughout this book, we've explored Ikigai in all its dimensions: its theory, its four foundational pillars, and its practical applications in daily life and times of crisis. We've seen how this Japanese philosophy can transform how we live, helping us find meaning not only in big goals but also in small, everyday actions.

1. The Power of Small Steps

Finding your Ikigai doesn't require revolutionizing your life overnight. Instead, lasting changes often begin with small gestures and actions that accumulate value over time. Whether it's spending a few minutes daily on something you love, taking care of your physical and mental well-being, or investing energy into relationships that make you feel connected, every effort counts.

Ikigai doesn't demand perfection but authenticity. Each small step toward what makes you feel alive and fulfilled contributes to your well-being and the world around you. This gradual and consistent commitment allows you to build a life filled with meaning and satisfaction.

2. Facing Challenges with Resilience

Your journey to Ikigai won't always be linear. Like any journey, you'll encounter obstacles, moments of uncertainty, and even failures. But it's in these challenges that Ikigai reveals its deepest value. When you know your purpose, you have an inner compass to guide you through the toughest storms.

We've explored how Ikigai can help you overcome stress, burnout, and uncertainties, providing practical tools and a holistic approach. Through mindfulness, gratitude, and the support of meaningful relationships, you can find the strength and motivation to move forward. Every crisis can become an opportunity to grow and bring you closer to your Ikigai.

3. Ikigai as a Contribution to the Greater Good

Your Ikigai isn't just about you; it's a thread connecting you to others and the world. When you live in alignment with your purpose, you inspire those around you to do the same. Your actions, no matter how small, can create a positive impact that extends beyond your personal life.

Whether it's helping a colleague, supporting an important cause, or sharing your talents with your community, every gesture in harmony with your Ikigai contributes to creating a happier and more balanced world. As we explored in the final chapters, Ikigai can be a transformative force for tackling global challenges, from sustainability to collective well-being. Each person living their purpose becomes a piece of a larger mosaic, contributing to a more harmonious and sustainable future.

4. The Journey Continues

Discovering your Ikigai is only the beginning. Once you start living according to this philosophy, you'll find that your purpose isn't static but evolves with you. Your passions, skills, and priorities may change over time, and Ikigai accompanies you in every stage, adapting to your needs and experiences.

Keep exploring, learning, and experimenting. Listen to yourself and the world around you. Remember that Ikigai isn't a final destination but a journey that allows you to grow and continuously discover new dimensions of yourself.

5. A Call to Action

As we conclude this book, I invite you to reflect on what you've learned and apply the principles of Ikigai in your daily life. Start with small steps: dedicate time to what you love, explore your talents, connect with others, and find ways to contribute to the world. Even the simplest actions, when guided by your Ikigai, can lead to great results.

I hope this journey through Ikigai has inspired you and given you the tools to create a more meaningful, happy, and balanced life. Your purpose is there, within you, ready to be discovered and lived.

Take the first step, with confidence and curiosity. Your Ikigai awaits.

Final Reflections and Encouragements

As we conclude this journey of discovering Ikigai, it's important to reflect on what you've learned and the potential now in your hands. Ikigai is not a magical formula but a valuable guide to living a more meaningful and fulfilling life. It invites you to look within, recognize your worth, and find a balance between your passions, skills, and what the world needs.

A Personal and Unique Journey

Your Ikigai is as unique as you are. No journey will be the same, and that's the beauty of this philosophy—it gives you the freedom to explore, experiment, and create your own path. What matters is not how quickly you find it, but the awareness and intentionality with which you live the process. Even small steps are significant strides toward a more fulfilling life.

Don't worry if your Ikigai doesn't become clear immediately. It's often a process of trial and error, continually adjusting your course. Every step, every lesson learned, and every moment of reflection brings you closer to your inner truth.

The Importance of Kindness Toward Yourself

On this journey, remember to be kind to yourself. There will be moments of doubt, uncertainty, and even frustration, but these are part of the process. Ikigai is not a rigid goal but a flexible guide that adapts to your experiences and changes. Allow yourself to make mistakes, to pause, and to pick up the path again when you're ready.

Remember, the value of your life isn't measured solely by achievements but by the quality of your daily moments, the authentic connections you create, and the meaning you find in the small things. Being present and mindful is already a significant step toward your Ikigai.

The Power of Inspiration

Your Ikigai doesn't just enrich you as an individual; it has the potential to inspire those around you. Living according to your purpose can become a source of positive energy for your friends, family, colleagues, and even your community. When you are authentic and aligned with what makes you happy, you encourage others to do the same.

Share your journey, experiences, and successes, even if they seem small. Telling your story can help others reflect on their own Ikigai and begin their journey. Every life lived with intention and passion has the power to create a ripple effect of positivity.

A Call to Action

Ultimately, the journey toward Ikigai requires action. It's not enough to reflect or dream—action transforms intuition into reality. I encourage you to begin today with a simple but meaningful gesture:

- Spend 10 minutes on an activity you truly love.
- Reflect on one aspect of your life you want to improve and commit to changing it.
- Take a small step to contribute to the well-being of others, whether through an act of kindness or support for a cause close to your heart.

It doesn't matter where you start—what matters is the decision to begin. Even the longest journey starts with a single step.

The Life You Want Awaits

Your life is a work of art that you have the power to shape. Every day offers you the opportunity to choose, act, and move closer to your Ikigai. No matter where you are now, your purpose is there, ready to be discovered, lived, and shared.

I leave you with this encouragement: embrace your journey with enthusiasm, courage, and openness. Find joy in the small things, be grateful for what you have, and look ahead with confidence. Your Ikigai is your gift, your guide, and your strength. Live it fully, and you will find that not only will your life become richer, but the world around you will become a better place thanks to your contribution.

Your journey toward Ikigai is just beginning.

Safe travels!

Appendix: Practical Exercises

Frequently Asked Questions About Ikigai

1.   What is Ikigai exactly?

Ikigai is a Japanese concept representing the reason you wake up every morning. It's the intersection of what you love, what you're good at, what the world needs, and what you can be paid for. It's not a rigid formula but a personal journey toward a meaningful life.

2.   Do I need to change careers to find my Ikigai?

Not necessarily. Ikigai can be found outside your profession. Many people discover their purpose through activities outside work, such as hobbies, volunteering, or meaningful relationships. If your current job doesn't fully align with your Ikigai, you can look for ways to integrate what you love into your daily life.

3. How long does it take to find my Ikigai?

There's no set timeline. For some, the journey to Ikigai can take years of exploration and reflection, while for others, it may emerge naturally. The key is to start with small steps and accept that the journey is as important as the destination.

4. Can my Ikigai change over time?

Yes, Ikigai can evolve as you grow and change as a person. Your passions, skills, and life circumstances may shift over time, leading you to redefine your purpose. What's important is to keep reflecting and adapting to what brings meaning to your life at different stages.

5. How can I start exploring my Ikigai?

You can begin by reflecting on the four fundamental components of Ikigai: your passions, your skills, the world's needs, and professional opportunities. Use the practical worksheets provided in this book to guide your reflection, and try to dedicate time daily to activities that resonate with you.

Ikigai Worksheets and Exercises

Below are simple, printable worksheets and exercises designed to help you explore and apply Ikigai in your life. Each sheet includes clear instructions and space for personal reflection.

1. Ikigai Reflection Map

Create a visual representation of your Ikigai by filling out a diagram with the following sections:

What you love

What you're good at

What the world needs

What you can be paid for

Instructions:

Write at least three ideas for each section.

Identify overlaps between sections to uncover potential areas of purpose.

Reflect on how these overlaps align with your current life.

2. Daily Ikigai Journal

Set aside 5-10 minutes daily to jot down:

One thing that made you feel alive or fulfilled today.

An action or decision you took that aligned with your values.

One step you can take tomorrow to move closer to your Ikigai.

3. Ikigai Action Plan

Develop a plan to incorporate Ikigai into your daily routine:

Choose one area of overlap in your Ikigai Map.

Write down three small actions to explore this area further.

Set a timeline for implementing these actions (e.g., within the next week or month).

4. Passion Discovery Exercise

Reflect on moments when you've felt most alive:

What were you doing?

Who were you with?

How did it make you feel?

What patterns do you notice?

5. Community Contribution Checklist

Explore how you can align your Ikigai with the needs of your community:

List three ways your skills or passions can help others.

Identify local groups, organizations, or causes that resonate with your values.

Commit to one act of service or contribution this month.

Final Note on Practical Application

Each worksheet is designed to help you take small, manageable steps toward living your Ikigai. Whether it's dedicating time to a beloved activity, exploring a new skill, or connecting with your community, every action brings you closer to a life filled with purpose and fulfillment.

Take your time, be patient with yourself, and enjoy the process of uncovering your unique Ikigai.

Printable Worksheets and Exercises

Ikigai Grid

Objective: Identify the four pillars of Ikigai and find their intersection.

Instructions:

Draw four overlapping circles on a blank sheet as follows:

Circle 1: "What you love" (Passion)

Write down everything that excites you and brings you joy.

Circle 2: "What you are good at" (Vocation)

List your skills and abilities.

Circle 3: "What the world needs" (Mission)

Reflect on ways you can contribute to improving society or the environment.

Circle 4: "What you can be paid for" (Profession)

Output:

The intersection of these four circles represents your Ikigai.

Day of the Week	Activities That Brought Me Joy	Challenges or Difficulties Faced	What I Learned About My Ikigai

Monday			
Tuesday			
Wednesday			
Thursday			
Friday			
Saturday			
Sunday			

Weekly Ikigai Journal

Objective: Track your progress toward Ikigai and reflect on your actions.

Instructions:

- At the end of each day, fill out this table by noting:

- - **Activities that brought you joy.**
  - **Moments of difficulty or challenges you encountered.**
  - **Insights about your Ikigai from the day's experiences.**
- At the end of the week, review your responses to identify patterns or areas for improvement.

1. Daily Completion:

    - At the end of each day, take a few minutes to fill out the worksheet:
    - Write down **activities** that brought you joy.
    - Note any **challenges or difficulties** you faced.
    - Reflect on and record **insights** about your Ikigai from the day's experiences.

2. Weekly Review:

    - At the end of the week:
    - Read through all your entries carefully.
    - Look for **patterns** in your responses (e.g., recurring sources of joy or repeated challenges).
    - Identify specific **areas for improvement** or adjustments to align your actions more closely with your Ikigai.

3. Apply Insights:

    - Based on your reflections, make intentional changes for the following week:
    - Focus more on activities that bring joy and align with your purpose.
    - Develop strategies to overcome recurring challenges.
    - Continue refining your understanding of your Ikigai.

This practice encourages mindfulness and continuous improvement, helping you to deepen your connection with your purpose over time.

List of Passions and Skills

Objective: Identify what you love to do and what you are good at.

Worksheet Layout: Divide the page into two columns:

- **Column 1:** "What I Love to Do." Write down everything that excites you and makes you feel alive, even if it seems unrelated to work.

- **Column 2:** "What I Am Good At." List the skills you have developed in life, both personal and professional.

Exercise: Once completed, look for connections between the two columns and circle the items that overlap.

What I Love to Do	What I Am Good At

Planning Your Ikigai Routine

Objective: Create a daily routine that supports your purpose.

Worksheet Layout: Divide the page into three sections:

1. **Morning:** What habits can you introduce to start your day with energy and positivity? (Example: meditation, exercise, reading).

2. **Afternoon:** Activities that keep you productive and aligned with your Ikigai. (Example: working on a project you are passionate about).

3. **Evening:** Practices to relax and reflect on the day. (Example: writing a gratitude journal).

Exercise: Plan your week and try to follow the routine. At the end, reflect on how it made you feel.

Morning	Afternoon	Evening

Life Balance Exercise

Objective: Assess your current balance among the four pillars of Ikigai.

Worksheet Layout: Draw a square divided into four sections:

- **Passion** (What you love)

- **Vocation** (What you are good at)

- **Mission** (What the world needs)

- **Profession** (What you can be paid for)

Exercise:

1. Rate your level of satisfaction in each area on a scale of 1 to 10.

2. Shade or fill the sections based on your score. (For example, if Passion is 8 out of 10, fill in 80% of its section.)

3. Review your balance and reflect on which area needs more attention..

Passion

(What you are good at)

Vocation

(What you love)

Mission   Profession

(What the world needs)   (What you can be paid for)

World Needs Map

Objective: Identify how you can contribute to the collective good.

Sheet Layout:

- At the center, write "What does the world need?"
- Draw branches around the central circle, like a mind map.

Main Branches:

- Local Community
- Environment
- Interpersonal Relationships
- Work Sector

Exercise:

- Write ideas for each branch and try to identify at least one concrete action you can take.

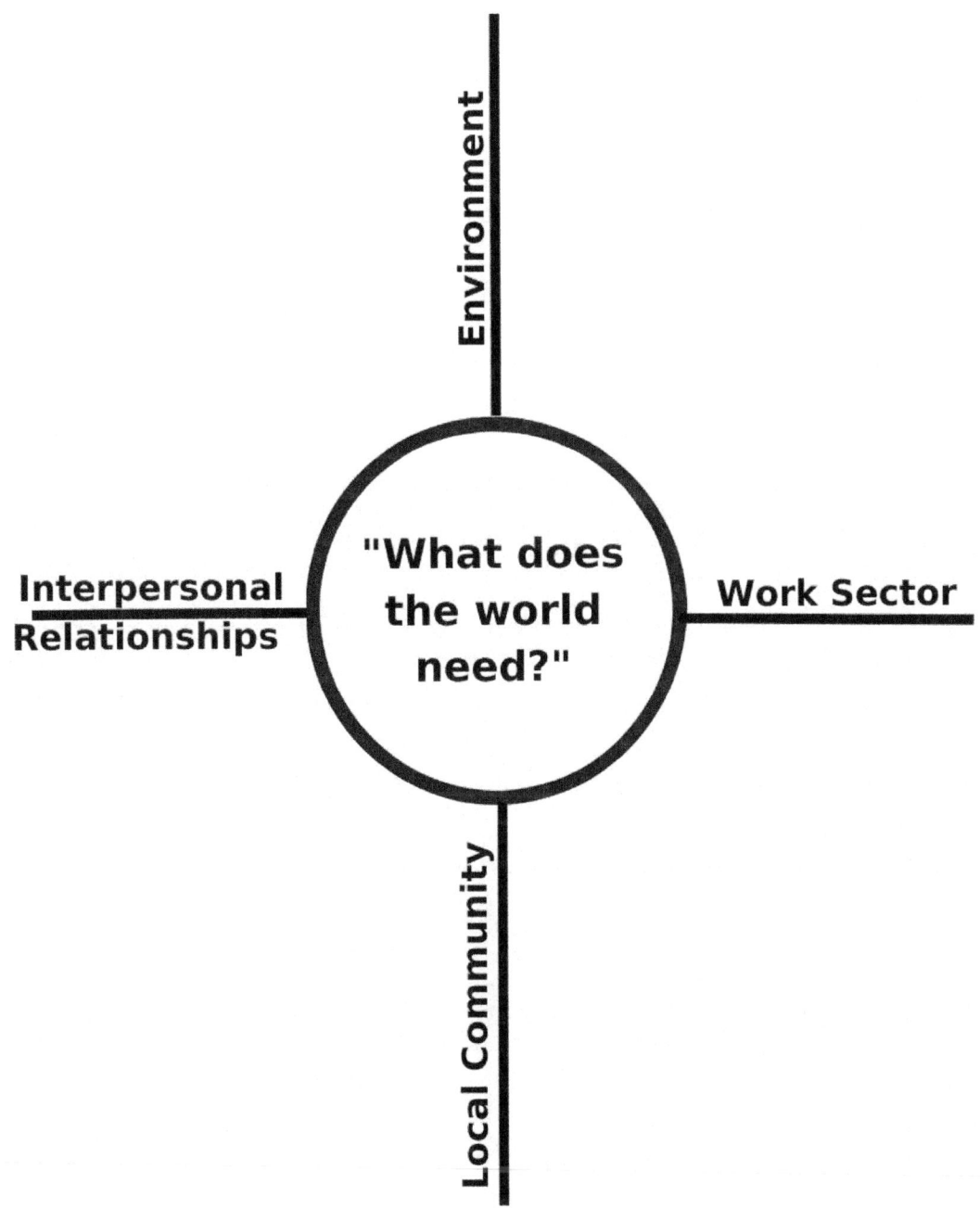

Gratitude and Mindfulness

Objective: Cultivate mindfulness and gratitude to support your Ikigai.

Sheet Layout:

- **Section 1**: "3 Things I'm Grateful for Today."
- (Example: a meaningful conversation, a moment of peace, a personal success).

- **Section 2**: "1 Moment When I Felt Fully Present."

(Example: a walk, reading a book, a deep conversation).

Instructions: Fill out this sheet every evening for a week and reflect on how it changes your perspective.

Three Things I'm Grateful for Today	One Moment When I Felt Fully Present

Finding Connections Between the Pillars

Objective: Identify how the four pillars of Ikigai intersect in your life.

Sheet Layout: Draw four columns:

- **What You Love.**

- **What You Are Good At.**

- **What the World Needs.**

- **What You Can Be Paid For.**

Exercise: Write ideas or examples under each column and try to identify areas of overlap. These intersections represent potential pathways to your Ikigai.

What You Love	What You Are Good At	What the World Needs	What You Can Be Paid For

Analytical Index

Theoretical Part 5
The Theory of Ikigai 6
   A Timeless Concept 9
   Ikigai and Happiness: A Different Approach 9
   Ikigai: A Compass for Modern Life. 10
   Ikigai as a Japanese Philosophy of Life 10
   Ikigai and Intentional Living 10
   Ikigai and the Importance of Community 11
   Ikigai and Simplicity 11
   Ikigai and Resilience 11
   Ikigai and the Balance of Mind, Body, and Spirit 12
   Why Ikigai is Important in Modern Society 13
   The Absence of Purpose: A Problem of Our Time 13
   Ikigai and Work: A New Perspective 13
   The Need for Connection and Belonging 14
   Ikigai and Mental Well-Being: An Antidote to Stress 14
   Ikigai and Sustainability: A Model for the Future 15
   What You Love to Do (Passion) 17
   Passion as Vital Energy 17
   Discovering What You Love to Do 17
   The Challenges of Cultivating Passion 18
   Passion and Meaning 18
   Contribution to the Well-Being of Others 19
   The Multiplier Effect of Passion 20

Overcoming Difficulties Through Passion 20
Integrating Passion Into Daily Life 20

What You're Good At (Vocation) 21
The Connection Between Talent and Vocation 21
Discovering What You're Good At 22
The Importance of Training and Practice 23
Stepping Outside Your Comfort Zone 23
Putting Vocation at the Service of Others 24
Vocation and Personal Fulfillment 24
Vocation as an Expression of Potential 25
The Role of Vocation in Overcoming Challenges 25
Vocation and Sense of Belonging 26
Vocation and Long-Term Fulfillment 26
What the World Needs (Mission) 27
Balancing the Personal and the Collective 29
Examples of Missions in Daily Life 29
Helping Others Through Your Work 29
Volunteering 30
Education and Sharing 30
Environmental Sustainability 30
The Connection Between Mission and Happiness 31
What You Can Be Paid For (Profession) 32
Profession as an Expression of Your Value 32
How to Find a Profession Aligned with Your Ikigai 33
The Importance of Economic Sustainability 34
Challenges and Opportunities in Finding the Right 34

Profession 34

Integrating Profession Into Your Ikigai 35

How These Elements Intertwine in Your Life 35

Key Questions to Explore Your Ikigai 36

The Process of Finding Balance..36

The Heart of Ikigai: Balancing the Internal and External 37

The Dynamic Between Passion and Vocation 37

   Conclusion 37

The Connection Between Mission and Profession 38

When the Pillars Are Out of Balance 38

Invest in Personal Development 39

Integrating the Pillars Into Daily Life 40

Seek Opportunities for Alignment...41

Commit to Personal Growth 41

Find Meaning in Small Gestures 42

Inner Harmony: Living in Balance with Oneself..............................45

What Is Inner Harmony? 45

The Role of Self-Awareness 45

Cultivating Balance in Everyday Life 46

The Connection Between Ikigai and Resilience 47

Inner Harmony and Relationships 48

The Journey Toward Inner Harmony 48

Happiness and Satisfaction: Finding Joy in Small Things...............48

The Japanese Concept of "Ikigai-kan"...49

The Connection Between Simplicity and Happiness.......................49

The Role of Gratitude in Daily Satisfaction 50

The Importance of "Here and Now" 50

Shared Happiness: The Power of Relationships 50

Incorporating Ikigai into Your Daily Life 51

Longevity and Well-being: The Secret of Okinawa's Inhabitants 52

The Connection Between Ikigai and Longevity 52

A Balanced Lifestyle 53

Balanced Diet and Moderation 53

Natural and Consistent Physical Activity 53

Meaningful Relationships 53

Rituals and Gratitude 53

The Mind-Body Connection 54

Lessons from Ikigai for the Modern World 54

Find a Meaningful Activity 54

Cultivate Authentic Relationships 55

Find Moments of Stillness 55

Incorporating Okinawa's Principles into Modern Life 56

Stories of People Who Embody Ikigai 58

The Wisdom of Longevity: Haru, the Farmer from 58

Okinawa 58

Mastery of Traditional Art: Keiko, the Ceramicist 58

A Sense of Belonging: Hiroshi, the Fisherman from Hokkaido 59

Caring for Others: Emi, the Pediatric Nurse 59

Teaching the Next Generation: Takeshi, the Calligraphy Master 60

Connections with Other Japanese Philosophies: 61

Wabi-Sabi, Zen, Kaizen 61

Wabi-Sabi: The Beauty of Imperfection 61

Zen: Presence in the Moment 61

Kaizen: Continuous Improvement 62

Applying These Philosophies to Daily Life 63

Ikigai and Social Connections: The Value of Belonging 64

The Importance of Social Bonds in Japanese Culture 65

Ikigai as a Contribution to Others 65

Relationships as the Foundation of Ikigai 65

The Power of Small Actions 66

Lessons for the Modern World 66

Fears and Insecurities: How to Overcome Them 69

Practical Tools to Face Your Fears 70

The "I Don't Have Time" Syndrome 72

The Myth of Not Having Enough Time 72

Recognizing True Priorities 73

Managing Distractions 73

Learning to Say No 74

Creating an Intentional Routine 74

> Conclusion 74

The Influence of Society and External Expectations 75

How to Free Yourself from External Expectations 76

Facing Others' Judgments 77

Surround Yourself with the Right People 77

Reconnecting with Your Ikigai 77

Exercises to Reflect on What You Love to Do 81

Identifying Your Talents and Skills 84

The Connection Between Talent and Ikigai 84

Connecting Talents to Your Ikigai 87

Overcoming Insecurities About Your Abilities 87

Recognizing the Needs of the World Around You 88

Why Recognizing the World's Needs Is Important 89

Why Recognizing the World's Needs Is Important 89

How to Identify the World's Needs 89

Connecting Your Talents to the Needs of the World 91

Overcoming Challenges in Addressing the World's Needs 91

Understanding the Intersection of the Four Pillars 93

The Risk of Imbalance 94

Accepting That Balance Can Change 95

Ikigai Journal: How to Track Your Progress 100

Using the Journal to Overcome Challenges 102

Long-Term Benefits of the Journal 103

Daily Practices of Mindfulness and Gratitude 103

Daily Mindfulness Practices 105

Daily Gratitude Practices 106

Combining Mindfulness and Gratitude 107

How to Build Routines That Reflect Your Ikigai 109

Practical Routines to Support Your Ikigai 109

Building Meaningful Relationships Based on Your Values 126

Rediscovering Your Purpose After Failure or Major Change 145

Applying Ikigai to Sustainability and Collective 160

Well-being 160

The Journey Toward Your Ikigai: A Unique and Personal Path 165

Printable Worksheets and Exercises 173

Analytical Index 192

Printed in Great Britain
by Amazon